Marie A. Shipley

The Icelandic Discoverers of America

Honour to whom honour is due

Marie A. Shipley

The Icelandic Discoverers of America
Honour to whom honour is due

ISBN/EAN: 9783337196233

Printed in Europe, USA, Canada, Australia, Japan

Cover: Foto ©ninafisch / pixelio.de

More available books at **www.hansebooks.com**

CHURCH DOOR AT VALTHIOF STAD, ICELAND, ELEVENTH CENTURY.
Frontispiece.

THE ICELANDIC DISCOVERERS

OF AMERICA;

OR,

HONOUR TO WHOM HONOUR IS DUE.

BY

MARIE A. BROWN,

AUTHOR OF "THE SUNNY NORTH, OR, SWEDEN OF THE PAST AND OF THE PRESENT,"
"NORWAY AS IT IS;" AND TRANSLATOR OF "THE SURGEON'S STORIES,"
"NADESCHDA," THE "SCHWARTZ" NOVELS, ETC.

"'They called the country Vinland.'
"'We know it,' said I. 'I am a Vinlander.'"
BAYARD TAYLOR.

BOSTON:
MARIE A. BROWN.
1888.

CONTENTS.

CHAPTER I.
THE IMMEDIATE NECESSITY OF ESTABLISHING THE TRUTH   PAGE 1

CHAPTER II.
THE MANIFEST DUTY OF THE UNITED STATES IN THIS QUESTION 35

CHAPTER III.
THE EVIDENCE THAT THE ICELANDERS DISCOVERED AMERICA IN THE TENTH CENTURY. 58

CHAPTER IV.
ROMAN CATHOLIC COGNIZANCE OF THE FACT AT THE TIME OF THE ICELANDIC DISCOVERY. 70

CHAPTER V.
ALL THE MOTIVES FOR THE CONCEALMENT AND FRAUD . 77

CHAPTER VI.
COLUMBUS' VISIT TO ICELAND. 100

CHAPTER VII.
THE SCANDINAVIAN NORTH AND SPAIN CONTRASTED . 111

CHAPTER VIII.

The Norse Discoverers and Columbus Contrasted . 147

CHAPTER IX.

The Beneficial Results to the Present Age and Posterity of Attributing this Momentous Discovery to the True Persons 165

CHAPTER X.

The Celebration of it in 1985! . . 185

CHAPTER XI.

The Righted Position of the Scandinavian North after this Justice has been accorded to it . 195

Bibliography of the important Books confirming the Icelandic Discovery of America, from the years 1076–1883 209

THE
ICELANDIC DISCOVERERS OF AMERICA;

OR,

HONOUR TO WHOM HONOUR IS DUE.

CHAPTER I.

THE IMMEDIATE NECESSITY OF ESTABLISHING THE TRUTH.

AND why the *immediate* necessity, it may be asked, of establishing a truth that has been hidden for a thousand years? The Norse discovery has been buried in antiquity for a millenary; admitting that it was an actual discovery, it was made by men of an ancient race that are now extinct; they turned it to no practical account and it led to no practical results. Moreover, the accounts of it are too vague and unauthentic to have been made a matter of veritable history; we have all been taught that Columbus discovered America, and it is very hard to disabuse our minds of that idea.

These are the current remarks and objections that greet the unlooked-for assertion that the *Norsemen* discovered America. They are also followed by the assumption that it is a matter of no importance either way, and may be left to antiquarians, if they choose to occupy themselves with this obscure question.

Following out this conclusion, if it is indeed a matter of no importance whether the Norsemen discovered America or not, it becomes equally unimportant whether Columbus discovered

America or not, and the discovery of the western continent ceases to be one of the greatest of events. That it has not been considered a trifling incident, or a mere matter of accident that posterity could not be expected to bear in mind, is proven by the extreme attention history has devoted to it, and the fame that the world, at the bidding of the imperative mandate of history, has accorded to Columbus, as a man who has accomplished an unparalleled achievement. If this fame is rightfully due to Columbus, on the assumption that he discovered America, if the magnitude of the achievement is not exaggerated, if it was an herculean undertaking to cross the ocean on such a quest in those days, if Columbus should enjoy the homage of centuries in the past and of centuries to come, then the same fame is rightfully due to the Norsemen, on the assumption that *they* discovered America, the magnitude of the achievement being greater in their case, inasmuch as it was accomplished five hundred years before Columbus planned his enterprise, and thus presupposes men five hundred years in advance of him in intelligence, courage, and nautical information and skill, and from the additional fact that this was only one of many undertakings on their part, for the settlement and colonization of new and far-off lands, if not their discovery, was an every-day affair with them. The lofty pride of the Norsemen, even more than humility, would for ever have prevented them from boasting of the discovery as did Columbus: "But our Redeemer hath granted this victory to our illustrious king and queen and their kingdoms, which have acquired great fame by an event of such high importance in which all Christendom ought to rejoice, and which it ought to celebrate with great festivals and the offering of solemn thanks to the Holy Trinity with many solemn prayers, both for the great exaltation which may accrue to them in turning so many nations to our holy faith, and also for the temporal benefits which will bring great refreshment and gain, not only to Spain, but to all Christians." He wrote besides:

"I gave to the subject six or seven years of great anxiety, explaining to the best of my ability, how great service might be done to our Lord, by this undertaking, in promulgating His sacred name and our holy faith among so many nations; an enterprise so exalted in itself, and so calculated to enhance the glory and immortalize the renown of great sovereigns." And one who edited an edition of Columbus' letters, says in his introduction: "The entire history of civilization presents us with no event, with the exception perhaps of the art of printing, so momentous as the discovery of the western world." But to a race who had founded the empire of Russia, the republics of Switzerland and Iceland, who had conquered Normandy and Great Britain, keeping a line of kings on the thrones of England and France, as they kept their czars on the throne of Russia, who "revived Hannibal's exploits in Italy," and shaped the confines of that land,—to such a race the discovery *even of America* was not an achievement so much more dazzling than the rest of their mighty deeds, while to Columbus it was the only thing he ever did.

The scope of the Norse undertakings can best be judged by a perusal of the words of the Swedish historian, Strinnholm, on the subject: "It seems wonderful how the fleets and hosts of the North could be sufficient to embrace the whole stretch of coast from the Elbe clear to the Pyrenese peninsula, and for a whole generation not only keep the lands lying along the whole coast in a constant state of siege, but also to extend their expeditions to the Mediterranean, clear to the coast of Italy, and yet during the same time the British Isles, England, Ireland and Scotland, continued to be hard pressed by the hosts from the North."

Columbus' estimate, however, of the value of the discovery of the "New World," was not extravagant; none know so well the value of a thing as the one who appropriates it wrongfully, and the usurper is a good judge of the territory he invades

"A practised slave-dealer," as Arthur Helps styles him, the commercial faculty was largely developed in him, much more largely than respect for the rights of property; he possessed himself of the coveted acquisition of the Northmen, robbed them of their discovery, with the same ease and with as little compunction as he kidnapped slaves. Note a little suggestion of his to their "highnesses" in Spain, this likewise for the enhancement of their greatness and the glory of the Lord: "Considering what great need we have of cattle and of beasts of burthen, both for food and to assist the settlers on this and all these islands, both for peopling the land and for cultivating the soil, their Highnesses might authorize a suitable number of caravels to come here every year to bring over the said cattle, and provisions and other articles; these cattle, &c., might be sold at moderate prices for account of the bearers, and the latter might be paid with slaves, taken from among the Carribees, who are a wild people, fit for any work, well proportioned and very intelligent, and who, when they have got rid of the cruel habits to which they have become accustomed, will be better than any other kind of slaves." Commenting upon this, Arthur Helps says: "At the same time that we must do Columbus the justice to believe that his motives were right in his own eyes, it must be admitted that a more distinct suggestion for the establishing of a slave-trade was never proposed." These slaves which he stole were to be exchanged for cattle and other necessaries; the discovery that he stole was to be converted into honours, wealth, distinction, an undying fame and saintship for himself! He wielded a lucid and persuasive, as well as pious pen, one that secured spiritual and temporal ends with equal facility, and he represented adequately and explicitly the value of this vast territorial acquisition, which he claimed as his discovery, to both Church and Throne. His own words yield the best testimony. After reading this self-laudation, what an unconscious satire appear the words of William Robertson, in his "History of America," when describing this man: "Columbus, in whose character the modesty and diffidence of true genius was united with the ardent enthusiasm of a projector." But Columbus has a modern admirer and biographer who has struck his own key and inflection, and who both revives and perpetuates the fame of the long-suffering exile from predestined bliss, by building his "Life of Columbus" on the eminently pious one of Roselly de Lorgues, from which it is compiled; this Catholic author, J. J. Barry, extols, with the rhapsody of the faithful, "the immortal discoverer of America, who, it is to be hoped, will ere long be solemnly enrolled on the glorious catalogue of the canonized saints."

That Columbus' words were entirely convincing to the Church, is proven by the fact that "Pope Alexander VI. (Roderigo Borgia) deeded the continent of America to Spain, solely on the statement of Columbus," as quoted by Aaron Goodrich in his work "History of the Character and Achievements of the so-called Christopher Columbus." This trenchant author, who dissects Columbus' character in the most unsparing way, also cites Count Roselly de Lorgues on the above point: "The pope has faith in Columbus. He yields full credence to him and justifies his calculations. *It is solely on Columbus that he depends; it is relying on Columbus that he engages in the vast partition of the unexplored world, between the crowns of Spain and Portugal. Everything the messenger of the cross proposes is granted in full, as a thing that is indicated by Providence.*" "To attack the latter was, therefore," comments Goodrich, "to attack the justice of the pope's bull, and an indirect imputation on papal infallibility. . . . In Spain it became necessary for all who would write a history of the New World to extol Columbus and the Church."

In the "Memorials of Columbus," a collection of authentic documents, whose value is glowingly stated by the one who edited them and wrote the historical memoir, D. Gio. Batista

Spotorno, as "a treasure which contains the diplomatic history of the discovery of America, and of Christopher Columbus; that is, of the most memorable event which had occurred for ages, and of a hero who reflects the highest honour on Genoa, on Italy, and on Europe,"—in this book will be found the famous Bull, of which the following is an extract: "And in order that you may undertake more freely and boldly the charge of so great an affair, given to you with the liberality of apostolic grace, We of our own motion, and not at your solicitation, nor upon petition presented to us upon this subject by other persons in your name, but of our pure will and certain knowledge, and with the plenitude of apostolic power, by the authority of God omnipotent granted to Us through blessed Peter, and of the vicarship of Jesus Christ, which we exercise upon earth, by the tenor of the presents, give, concede and assign for ever to you, and to the kings of Castile and Leon, your successors, all the islands and mainlands discovered and which may hereafter be discovered, towards the west and south, with all their dominions, cities, castles, places and towns, and with all their rights, jurisdictions, and appurtenances, whether the lands and islands found, or that shall be found, be situated towards India, or towards any other part whatsoever; and we make, constitute and depute you, and your aforesaid heirs and successors, lords of them, with full, free and absolute power and authority and jurisdiction: drawing, however, and fixing a line from the Arctic pole, viz., from the north, to the antarctic pole, viz., to the south; which line must be distant from any one of the islands whatsoever, vulgarly called the Azores and Cape de Verde islands, a hundred leagues towards the west and south—"

It will be gratifying to Americans to see the disposition that was made of their country; a disposition that the Roman Catholic power evidently regards as final and irrevocable. The author before quoted, Barry, may, I think, be said to interpret the views of the Romish hierarchy, when he reasons that "the question is not concerning an international interest, or of an affair to regulate for Castile, but about interests of vital importance to Catholicity, to the salvation of souls, and to the extension of the kingdom of Jesus Christ. . . . And here we see visibly," he continues, " the participation of the Church in the discovery, and where we perceive her agency, in the benediction given by Innocent III. to the enterprise of his countryman. . . . Rome comprehended Columbus. Now to comprehend is, in a certain sense, to become equal to. All the sympathies of the Holy Father and of the Sacred College, were in favour of Columbus." That these "sympathies" remain unchanged, is shown by his further words, as well as by a mass of outside evidence: " When lately in Rome we rendered homage to the moral and religious purity of Columbus, and declared his grandeur, our voice received, in the places of the pontificate, only friendliness and encouragement." Without substantial support from head-quarters, unless he was acting with a warrant, he could scarcely proceed with so much confidence and affirm: " Evidently God chose Columbus as a messenger of salvation;" and "The time for his historic rehabilitation has come at last," removing all uncertainty and suspense on this head by declaring at once: " The necessity of a new, full and complete history of the New World has been much felt; this necessity, which so much resembles a duty, has been deeply felt in the Eternal City; and we proceed to respond to it." Not content with saying that " it is too much forgotten that the work effected by Columbus is unequaled in history," he reaches a Roman Catholic climax by exclaiming: " We declare before God, who knows it, and before men, who do not know it, that CHRISTOPHER COLUMBUS WAS A SAINT."

In the words that the late King Alfonso is reported to have uttered in course of conversation with Clarence Winthrop Bowen, we see that the modern estimate of an occupant of the Spanish throne coincides perfectly with the joint estimate of Spain and Rome in the past, in regard to the immense value of this discovery. The two persons mentioned were speaking about the four hundredth anniversary of the discovery of America by Columbus, and the king thought that nine years was a long time to spend in arranging for the celebration, but perhaps not too long considering its importance. "It is an event," he said, "in which all the world would be interested, and in which the leading nations might unite. I would do all in my power to make it a brilliant festival; but, considering the pre-eminent part that Spain took in the discovery of America, I claim that she should certainly be allowed to have the celebration within her own borders. Italy gave birth to Columbus, it is true. Other countries considered his ideas only visionary schemes. But it was Spain alone that furnished the means for carrying into practical effect what would otherwise have been only a dream. To Spain alone, therefore, belongs the credit of the discovery."

A few panegyrics of Columbus by modern authors and historians may appropriately be culled and laid before the reader, as further evidence of the value ascribed to this discovery, for it is obvious that Columbus is extolled solely for that, and that his elevation from obscurity is due to that one achievement alone.

In Bancroft's "History of the United States" stand the words: "The enterprise of Columbus, the most memorable maritime enterprise in the history of the world, formed between Europe and America the communication that will never cease." Arthur Helps, in his "Life of Columbus," says that "perhaps there are few of the great personages in history who have been more talked about and written about than Christopher Columbus, the discoverer of America." To quote another passage of his: "Modern familiarity with navigation renders it difficult for us to appreciate adequately the greatness of the enterprise which was undertaken by the discoverers of the New World." But the writer obviously fails to see that the ancient familiarity with navigation, as evinced by the Norsemen, rendered it surprising and well-nigh incomprehensible that Columbus could have encountered so much difficulty in finding ships, crews, the necessary outfit for a voyage, and in managing the undertaking. The accounts read as if this might have been the first voyage on record, from any port; as risky, altogether, as the first balloon ascension.

Washington Irving, in his "Life of Columbus," in describing Columbus' state, after land had been descried, on that first voyage, remarks: "He had secured himself a glory which must be as durable as the world itself," but it is not quite plain whether this is the author's reflection or Columbus', or a blending of the two.

But for Christopher Columbus substitute the Norsemen; for Spain substitute the Scandinavian North; for the date 1492 substitute the dates 982-85; for San Salvador and San Domingo substitute Greenland, Labrador, Nova Scotia, Rhode Island, and Massachusetts; for a discoverer of two islands, who did not explore the mainland to any extent, substitute the discoverers who traversed the eastern coast of America from Labrador to Florida, just as their forefathers had traversed the western coast of Europe from the Hebrides to Africa; for a discoverer who stole his information, thus buying himself name and repute at the Spanish court, and who went to America in search of gold and slaves, also to appropriate new territory for the preaching of the Gospel, substitute the genuine discoverers, who were adepts in the art of navigation, who had already established so many colonies and formed so many governments that this had become an old story to them, and who being above the incentives of lucre and Papal patronage, devoted themselves to industry, commerce between the newly discovered continent, Greenland, Iceland, and Scandinavia, and such a thorough and intelligent exploration of it as to rouse the cupidity of southern Europe, five hundred years after their discovery, when an opportunity offered in the person of Columbus, for its states to avail themselves of it, and to confirm the fact of their prior discovery, in documents so reliable and authentic as to convince the modern world, after three hundred years of systematic concealment, of garbled history and fraud on the part of the Roman Catholic Church and its adherents; and when these substitutions are made, does the value of the discovery become less? Does it not rather become greater as showing how deeply those wearing the mantle of holiness, as well as the royal purple, have been willing to perjure themselves for the gains? And these men have intoned for ages: " Beware of covetousness ! " Is it the duty of all " the leading nations to unite," to use King Alfonso's words, to celebrate this fraud of half a millenary's duration, and by publicly recognizing the claim of Columbus' discovery gratify the covetousness of the Mother Church by turning the American Republic over to it, as its spiritual and temporal property ?

A moment's attention to another reading of this fact in history, from a northern instead of a southern standpoint, will show that the discovery in itself loses nothing by a change of characters. In the first part of the latest history of Sweden, under the joint authorship of Drs. Montelius and Hildebrand, Professors Weibull, Alin, Boethius, and others, there occurs this passage, from the pen of Dr. Oscar Montelius : " We have seen how the Northerners, during the Viking period, carried their victorious arms to most of the countries of Europe. All the intercourse between the North and the rest of the world during this time, however, was not warlike, for peaceful commerce was even then of an importance, which one has been but too much inclined to under-estimate. Foremost among peaceful voyages during the Viking period must we remember the bold voyages of discovery which the Norsemen then made. Already have we mentioned how they settled Iceland; from there they found first Greenland and afterwards Vinland, or the north-eastern part of what we now call the United States of America. To the Northmen is due the great glory, so far as history knows, of having first, among all the people of Europe, discovered America, and it was half a millenary before the inhabitants of southern Europe found their way to the new world, possibly led there by the *sagor* of the Norsemen's voyages."

Another Swedish historian, A. E. Holmberg, in his "Norsemen during the Pagan Period," ascribes the same glory to the discovery: "The treatise on the naval operations of our forefathers we can scarcely end more suitably than with the mention of their most daring naval exploit—an event, which not only in and of itself, but also through its results, shrewdly concealed until our time, is of world-historic importance, I mean *the discovery of America by the Norsemen toward the close of* 900. The matter, it is true, was some years ago explained and made known; the details of it, however, may in general be less known. From childhood we have all heard that the discovery of the new world was exclusively Columbus' exploit. His glory in defying prejudices and overcoming the difficulties and obstacles that rose against such an undertaking no people and no age can diminish; but nevertheless, the discovery of this world was never *his;* the glory of this belongs to the Norsemen alone."

Or if we turn to English authors, Wheaton, Laing, Pigott, Beamish, the Howitts, Carlyle, all credit the fact of the Norse discovery, and several of them, together with Scandinavian writers and historians of note, give so much testimony with regard to Columbus' visit to Iceland, that I reserve the important passages relating to this secret visit of the ambitious and unscrupulous southerner, so pregnant with results, for the chapter that is to treat of it exclusively. The third chapter contains the evidence of the Norse discovery, taken from as many authors as has been found practicable, and giving the opinions that are of the most value on this important subject. For the sources of all the knowledge that has as yet been derived, the reader is referred to the bibliography at the end of this book.

The American author, Aaron Goodrich, traces the sequence between the greatness of the true discoverers and the greatness of their discovery, showing that one was attributable to the other: "While the greater part of Europe was plunged in the intellectual darkness which pervaded the middle ages, while the monk in his cloister toiled laboriously during a life-time to perpetuate some one work of saintly or classic lore, and the masses were ignorant, superstitious, the slaves of feudal lords and barons scarcely less ignorant than themselves, a people flourished in the extreme north, with whom enterprise and freedom were neither dead nor stagnant, who possessed scientific knowledge and applied the same to practical purposes; a people simple, fearless and energetic, republicans in practice if not in name, with whom chieftains were the fathers and protectors of their followers, sharing their perils and respecting their rights; a pagan people indeed, worshippers of Odin and Thor, believers in the joys of Walhalla, yet doers of deeds so noble as to be worthy the most enlightened Christian: such were the Northmen; such their simple records, which bear every impress of truth, prove them to have been. Issuing from an Asiatic hive, they early overran Norway and Sweden; their language, the old Danish or *Dänsk tunga*, is now preserved only in Iceland, which they colonized in the year 875; in 985 they rediscovered and colonized Greenland; the same year the American continent proper was discovered by them, and, during the first years of the eleventh century, they made thither frequent voyages, residing, for periods of several years, at different times, in what is now called New England."

The Norwegian-American writer, Professor R. B. Anderson, in his stirring book "America not Discovered by Columbus," traces this sequence still further, namely, to the result that has now become the modern point of issue, the Columbian or bogus discovery, which was based upon the Norse one : " It was the first settlement of Iceland by the Norsemen, and the constant voyages between this island and Norway, that led to the discovery, first of Greenland and then of America ; and it is due to the high intellectual standing and fine historical taste of the Icelanders that records of these voyages were kept, first to instruct Columbus how to find America, and afterward to solve for us the mysteries concerning the discovery of this continent."

It is indisputably true that the value of the discovery is sufficient to command the attention of all ages ; the truth as to the discoverer remains to be demonstrated, and that is the proud task of the present age, nay, of this coming year, for the American people should not let 1887, the year of the National Exhibition on *English* soil, draw to a close, without a national declaration of the truth of the discovery of their country by the Norsemen, a public acknowledgment of the debt of gratitude in which they stand to the Scandinavian North, for which they are indebted for the principles of liberty, " for the hardiest elements of progress in the United States," according to Benjamin Lossing, and an equally public repudiation of the false claim of Columbus, throwing off, with the same indignant scorn as once the Mother country, when it attempted oppression, the clutch of the Mother Church and its obedient vassal Spain, to whom the Republic can charge the slavery that blackened its annals as a nation for so many years, the terrible war arising from that pernicious system introduced by Spain and largely kept alive by the Roman Catholic democratic party, North and South, all this evil in the past, and to whom, in the future, it would inevitably owe its destruction as a nation, the subversion of its free Constitution, and its transformation into a huge benighted territory indistinguishable in its mental and moral attributes from *South America*, the southern half of what the Church of Rome fondly looks forward to as the Roman Catholic hemisphere,—if the claim that Columbus discovered America should be admitted by it, as a nation.

This is the reason why it is necessary for the truth, as to the discovery of America, to be established *immediately*. The near approach of the four hundredth anniversary of the landing and alleged discovery of Columbus, has revived the subject in the public mind and the floating rumours, occasionally taking a concrete form in the American newspapers, of a grand commemoration of the event, convert it into a subject that must soon be decided one way or the other, and the approaching date, October 12th, 1892, into the date of a most momentous decision, one that will fairly shake the world with its reverberation! This approaching anniversary of a fraudulent discovery, the resolution of the United States with regard to it, their celebration of it, or their refusal to celebrate it, will test the sincerity and earnestness of the work of which the year 1876 was the glorious centennial; it will decide whether the date 1892 is to obliterate the date 1776, whether the Government, claiming to be purely secular, which has from the hour the Constitution was framed refused to admit the word "God" into it, will then be willing to insert both God and Pope in it; whether the country that indignantly threw off all allegiance in 1776 will then yield allegiance to the foulest tyrant the world has ever had, the Roman Catholic power!

As straws show which way the wind blows, it is worth while to note these newspaper bits: "It is proposed to have a World's Fair in Chicago in 1892, in commemoration of the four hundredth anniversary of the landing of Columbus in America." Another scrap indicated that the matter of a celebration, of some kind, of this event was under consideration, in Washington. Another ran thus: "The Spaniards have not yet made up their minds how to celebrate the four hundredth anniversary of the sailing of Columbus;" which was controverted by the following programme: "It is proposed in Spain to start a fleet of ships, representing all maritime nations, from the little port of Palos, in Spain, on August 3rd, 1892, the four hundredth anniversary of the sailing of Columbus, and to have the fleet sail to San Salvador over the route taken by the great discoverer." Another significant scrap made its appearance in an editorial column: "As an inducement to celebrate the fourth centenary of Columbus' landing, Americans are offered a chance to gaze upon the identical chains with which Bobadella loaded the wrists of Columbus when the great seaman was sent back to Spain a prisoner in 1500. It is an Italian chevalier who owns these dumb but eloquent articles, and to secure them he made costly journeys to Spain and America. For twenty years he has kept the matter a profound secret, having personal reasons for this reticence. But now they will be shown, and managers of dime museums who know their business will take the hint."

But here is something that intimates the absolute destruction of the plans mentioned: "Just as we are talking about a celebration of the four hundredth anniversary of Columbus' discovery of land on the western hemisphere, some Danish ethnologists are trying to prove that the Genoese navigator had borrowed all he knew from an old Iceland manuscript of the seventh century,[1] in which this continent was fully described." The phrase "are trying to prove" hardly fits the case; the incontestable fact is that the "old Iceland manuscript" referred to is in the possession of the Danish Government, and that the Royal Society of Northern Antiquaries, in Copenhagen, have placed its contents before the modern world, in the splendid work "Antiquitates Americanæ," by Professor Rafn, in which the narratives of the Norse voyages to America, besides being reproduced in the old Icelandic, are rendered into the Latin and Danish languages. An English translation having been

[1] The wrong date.

made of these by North Ludlow Beamish, this in turn has been reproduced by the Prince Society in Boston, under the title: "Voyages of the Northmen to America," published in 1877. This is only one of several translations into English, so that the contents of that portion of the "Codex Flatoiensis" relating to the discovery of America is in reality accessible to all. In Samuel Laing's preliminary dissertation to his translation of the "Heimskringla," the famous chronicle of the kings of Norway written by Snorre Sturleson, which also contains, in the saga of Olaf Tryggvason, historical testimony of the discovery of America by the Northmen, is to be found an account of this priceless volume : 'The Flateyar Annall, or Codex Flatoiensis,' by far the most important of Icelandic manuscripts, takes its name from the island Flatö, in Bredefiord in Iceland, where it had been long preserved, and where Bishop Swendson of Skalholt purchased it, about 1650, from the owner Jonas Torfeson, for King Frederick III., giving in exchange for it the perpetual exemption from land-tax of a small estate of the owner. The manuscript is in large folio, beautifully written on parchment. On the first page stands : 'This book is owned by Ion Hakonson. Here are first songs; then how Norway was inhabited or settled ; then of Eric Vidforla (the far-traveled); thereafter of Olaf Tryggvason, and all his deeds ; then next the saga of King Olaf the Saint, with all his deeds and therewith the sagas of the Orkney Earls ; then the saga of Swerrer and thereafter the saga of Hakon the Old, with the sagas of King Magnus his son ; then are deeds of Einer Sokkeson of Greenland, thereafter of Helge and Ulf the Bad ; then begin annals from the time the world was made, showing all to the present time that is come. The priest Ion Thordarson has written from Eric Vidforla, and the two sagas of the Olafs ; and priest Magnus Thorhallsson has written from thence, and also what is written before, and has illuminated the whole. God Almighty and the Holy Virgin bless those who wrote, and him who dictated.' ... The Codex Flatoiensis is not an original work by one author, but a collection of sagas transcribed from older manuscripts, and arranged in so far chronologically that the accounts are placed under the reign in which the events they tell of happened, although not connected with it or with each other. Under the saga of Olaf Tryggvason are comprehended the sagas of the Feroe Islands; of the Vikings of Jomsburg; of Erik Red and Leif his son, the discoverers of Greenland and Vinland; and the voyages of Karlsefne to Vinland, and all the circumstances, true or false, of their adventures."

As for Columbus having "borrowed all he knew" from this old Icelandic manuscript, the same author, Laing, to whom the world is deeply indebted for enlightenment on this hidden history, has important testimony to give. "The discovery of America or Vinland, in the 11th century, by the same race of enduring, enterprising seamen, is not less satisfactorily established by documentary evidence than the discovery and colonization of Greenland; but it rests entirely upon documentary evidence, which cannot, as in the case of Greenland, be substantiated by anything to be discovered in America. ... All that can be proved, or that is required to be proved, for establishing the priority of the discovery of America by the Northmen, is that the saga or traditional account of those voyages in the 11th century was committed to writing at a known date, viz. between 1387 and 1395, in a manuscript of unquestioned authenticity, of which these particular sagas or accounts relative to Vinland form but a small portion; and that this known date was eighty years before Columbus visited Iceland to obtain nautical information, viz. in 1477, when he must have heard of this written account of Vinland; and it was not till 1492 that he discovered America. This simple fact established on documents altogether incontrovertible, is sufficient to prove all that is wanted to be proved, or can be proved, and is much more clearly and ably stated by Thormod Torfæus, the great antiquary of the last century, than it has been since, in his very rare little tract, 'Historia Vinlandiæ Antiquæ,' 1707."

A credibility is thus given to this one manuscript from the North, not only by Laing, but by Alexander von Humboldt and hosts of others, that the collective testimony of the south lacks: whole libraries of lives of Columbus and histories of the New World weigh as nothing against it. The intrinsic truth of its written words gain an absolute authority from the integrity of the race from which it issued. Iceland has been the island refuge of this truth; Iceland has preserved it sacredly, and now transmits it to the Republic that she, in her own palmiest days as a Republic, conduced to found.

American honour is at stake! It is a national obligation for the American Republic to proclaim this truth and to do it quickly. The freest country cannot obey the behest of the most slavish one! America and Spain cannot be linked together in eternal union! the land that is the synonym of progress bound to the land that is the synonym of decay! The germ of republicanism, of liberty, was planted in America by the North, the germ of slavery by the South, by Spain and the Church of Rome. Which germ shall be allowed to grow? *Both* cannot live on American soil! The history of Europe is the history of this conflict between the North and the South, between free-minded Scandinavia and the arch-tyrant Rome. In Europe Rome has virtually conquered, for it succeeded in converting or Christianizing all the nations that comprise Europe, including the Scandinavians, who offered the most stubborn resistance, but were finally obliged to succumb, albeit five hundred years after all the others had bowed under the yoke of Rome. The struggle is now to be continued in the United States. The double discovery of America is symbolical of this, and is also the signal for contention. The true discovery was by men from the North, and of that portion of the land lying in the north, the alleged or false discovery was by men from

Spain, and of islands south even of the continent. In the one case no appropriation, in the other an immediate deed of the land, nay, of the whole hemisphere, by the Pope to the Sovereigns of Spain. The Norsemen named the land after its good qualities, *Vinland;* the Spaniards, according to the base use they meant to make of it: "*The Land of the Holy Cross, or New World.*" The Spaniards intended America to be the empire of the Pope in a sense in which Europe had failed to be it, the perfection of the original design, matured in the second and third centuries, having been impaired by the pagans of the North. But the Norsemen were in their graves; the wholesale Christianizing of Scandinavia had put their very spirit, soul, in the grave. What a divine retribution it would be upon this impious race, according to the Catholic way of reasoning, to steal their discovery, appropriate the land that *they* had found and convert it into what Europe should have been, *would* have been, if Ferdinand and Isabella, Philip II., Charlemagne and a few others could have completed the work of exterminating heretics!

The Roman Catholic, J. J. Barry, unwraps the motive, the forced tendency, from all disguise, and says plainly: "The first object of the Discovery, disengaged from every human consideration, was, therefore, the glorification of the Redeemer and the extension of His Church. Historians have hitherto left this circumstance unnoticed, or in a state of vague confusion." The Protestant, Arthur Gilman, in his "History of the American People," poetizes on a well-worn theme, the expression of the facts of the case having been given by the other, for no one can know so well as a Roman Catholic what the intentions of the Holy See are with regard to the United States. To quote Gilman's words: "Among the great events that marked the world's revival from the sleep of the Dark Ages, none was more remarkable than the revelation of the American continent. From the moment when the ship of Columbus was sighted off the coast of Spain, bearing the proofs of his discovery, the name America became the synonym of wealth, of adventure, of freedom."

There is not the slightest warrant for coupling the words wealth, adventure (in the good sense) and freedom with the name of Columbus. Sterility, poverty, slavery have invariably followed in the wake of Rome and of Spain. They would have done so in this instance, the United States would have displayed the features of Spanish civilization, had it not been for the principles of freedom the Norsemen infused into English blood and which found their fullest expression in the American colonists, leading them to declare independence. But the American Republic has always been divided against itself: the northern states respected freedom, defended it for themselves and others; the southern states advocated slavery and fought for its preservation; we have the freedom-loving North and slavery-worshipping Spain again typified in Boston and New Orleans.

Samuel Laing sees clearly that these are the only two forces that have been at work in Europe, for spiritual and temporal supremacy, and he embodies one, the enslaving force, in the Romans, and the other, the freeing force, in the Scandinavians. His words convey the whole truth of the situation as regards the past: "Two nations only have left permanent impressions of their laws, civil polity, social arrangements, spirit, and character on the civilized communities of modern times—the Romans, and the handful of Northern people from the countries beyond the Elbe, which had never submitted to the Roman yoke, who, issuing in small, piratical bands from the 5th to the 10th century, under the names of Saxons, Danes, Northmen, plundered, conquered and settled on every European coast from the White Sea to Sicily." *What* impression was left he describes in a way that leaves no doubt: "Wheresoever these people from beyond the pale and influence of the old Roman empire, and of the later church empire of Rome, either settled, mingled or marauded, they have left permanent traces in society of their laws, institutions, character, and spirit. Pagan and barbarian as they were, they seem to have carried with them something more natural, something more suitable to the social wants of man, than the laws and institutions formed under the Roman power. What traces have we in Britain of the Romans? A few military roads, and doubtful sites of camps, posts, and towns—a few traces of public works, and all indicating a despotic military occupation of the country, and none a civilized condition of the mass of the inhabitants—alone remain in England to tell the world that here the Roman power flourished during 400 years." There was thus a despotic military occupation of the country; that there was a despotic spiritual occupation of the mind follows as a matter of course: "The history of modern civilization resolves itself, in reality, into the history of the moral influence of these two nations. All would have been Roman in Europe at this day in principle and social arrangement—Europe would have been, like Russia or Turkey, one vast den of slaves, with a few rows in its amphitheatre of kings, nobles, and churchmen, raised above the dark mass of humanity beneath them, if three boats from the north of the Elbe had not landed in Ebbsfleet, in the Isle of Thanet, 1400 years ago, and been followed by a succession of similar boat expeditions of the same people, marauding, conquering, and settling, during 600 years, viz. from 449 to 1066. All that men hope for of good government and future improvement in their physical and moral condition—all that civilized men enjoy at this day of civil, religious, and political liberty—the British constitution, representative legislature, the trial by jury, security of property, freedom of mind and person, the influence of public opinion over the conduct of public affairs, the Reformation, the liberty of the press, the spirit of the age—all that is or has been of value to man in modern times as a member of society either in Europe or in

America, may be traced to the spark left burning upon our shores by these Northern barbarians."

A strong and eloquent statement this, which should be written in letters of fire in every American heart, to inspire them with deep gratitude to their true ancestors—ancestors which England, as a nation, has never honoured properly, wherefore the duty has devolved upon Americans, who, being more nearly allied to the Norsemen in soul-qualities, can alone understand them and appreciate them as they deserve. That *they* were the first Europeans who landed on American shores was pregnant with good to us; *this* made "the name America the synonym of wealth, of adventure, of freedom," and not the false tidings borne by Columbus to Spain of a discovery of which he would have been incapable but for stolen information.

And the other force, which we can best recognize under the name, *Rome*, what had it accomplished? Let Dr. Felix Oswald tell: "A thousand years' interregnum of science, Faith usurping the throne of Reason, every branch of human knowledge withered by the poison of supernaturalism, literary activity limited to the production of homilies and miracle-legends, education devoted to the suppression of all natural instincts, and the substitution of submissive belief for the love of truth and free inquiry. Decadence of the fine arts, natural science merged in a deluge of superstition." I doubt if in the whole range of literature could be found a more accurate summing-up of the work wrought by these two forces than that presented by these authors. Dr. Oswald insists, and with right, that "the misery of the Middle Ages was due, not to the supernatural, but to the *anti-natural*, tendency of the Christian religion," affirming, most truly, that "the pagan gods were the deified powers of nature, the patrons of mariners, shepherds, and husbandmen," while "the Christian gods were the deified enemies of nature." The evil, as he shows, reached appalling proportions, for "on the altar of her anti-natural idol, the Christian Church has sacrificed the lives of eighteen millions of the noblest and bravest of our fellowmen." His great work, "The Secret of the East," is a complete revelation of the hideous results of this rule of darkness falsely called "the light of Christianity." "Has the rule of the Church," he asks, "furthered the moral progress of the forty generations whose wisest, manliest, noblest, and bravest men were systematically weeded out, to enforce the survival of idiots and hypocrites? For thirteen centuries, the rack, the stake, and the cross were leagued against nature and mankind.' Hallam more than confirms Oswald's assertions: "A cloud of ignorance overspread the whole face of the Church, hardly broken by a few glimmering lights, who owe almost the whole of their distinction to the surrounding darkness. . . . I cannot conceive of any state of society more adverse to the intellectual improvement of mankind than one which admitted no middle line between dissoluteness and fanatical mortifications. . . . No original writer of any merit arose; and learning may be said to have languished in a region of twilight for the greater part of a thousand years. . . . In 992, it was asserted that scarcely a single person was to be found, in Rome itself, who knew the first elements of letters. Not one priest of a thousand in Spain, about the age of Charlemagne, could address a common letter of salutation to another."

Nor was this all; not content with debasing and enfeebling the mind, the Romish religionists changed the very face of nature; this was to be made as arid and barren as the soul—the Christian revision of the Creator's work, for, as Oswald says, " the dogmas of the Christian Church have cost the world three million square miles of lands, which once were the garden spots of this earth, but which have been turned into deserts by the neglect of rational agriculture and the influence of a creed which laboured to withdraw the attention of mankind from secular to *post-mortem* concernments." In support of this statement he cites Professor Marsh: "The fairest and fruitfullest portions of the Roman Empire, precisely that portion of terrestrial surface, in short, which about the commencement of the Christian era, was endowed with the greatest superiority of soil, climate and position, which had been carried to the highest pitch of physical improvement—is now completely exhausted of its fertility. A territory larger than all Europe, the abundance of which sustained in bygone centuries a population scarcely inferior to that of *the whole Christian world at the present day*, has been entirely withdrawn from human use, or, at best, is thinly inhabited. . . . There are regions where the operation of causes, set in action by man, has brought the face of the earth to *a desolation almost as complete as that of the moon;* and though within that brief space of time which we call 'the historical period,' they are known to have been covered with luxuriant woods, verdant pastures and fertile meadows, they are now too far deteriorated to be reclaimable by man, nor can they become again fitted for his use except through great geological changes, or other agencies, over which we have no control. . . . Another era of equal improvidence would reduce this earth to such a condition of impoverished productiveness as to threaten the depravation, barbarism, and, perhaps, even the extinction of the human species."

But, reply many Americans, with "that sublime trust in the grand destiny of the American people" for which they are noted, this could never happen in the United States; Roman Catholics here are not what they are in Italy or Spain; the Romish Church itself is becoming permeated with the spirit of our American institutions, of freedom. This pleasant illusion, which, carried one degree farther, would invite the contagion of the spiritual Black Death that ravaged Europe for a thousand years, and left the taint of the foul disease in the mental organism of all descendants—has blinded American eyes to the fact that Roman Catholicism has already made terrible strides in the Republic, that the freedom of American institutions has incalculably favoured its advance, saving it the trouble of forcing its way with the sword, as it was compelled to do in Europe; it is securing a bloodless victory, and its exultation, although perhaps premature, is not altogether unfounded. This insolent power has certainly met with no rebuke from the people or Government of the United States, not the slightest check; its jesuits have not been expelled, its monasteries and ecclesiastical establishments have not been forbidden, nor its parochial schools closed; it enjoys the absolute freedom of the press, and its editors can boast openly of their speedy appropriation of the American Republic for the seat of Romish despotism; the ancient Greeks, the Moors, the Albigenses, the Saxons, the Scandinavians, all made resistance, the citizens of the United States make none. How shall the Roman Catholics construe this, if not favourably to their plans? Freedom to them is valueless from the American point of view, as the atmosphere that will alone admit of the growth of a great and powerful nation, founded in the highest principles of human right and justice, but inestimable as affording them the fullest opportunity to undermine this nation, and blast not only its hopes, but the hopes of the world. Seizing the United States, the Church of Rome can mock and defy all the states of Europe that have always prevented its complete temporal sovereignty. The progress it has already made is by no means to be despised; as a writer in the "Boston Transcript" laments: "We look with dismay upon the appearance in our streets of fat, heavy-eyed priests and coifed nuns;" from having had, at the end of the last century—to quote some statistics given by an orthodox Russian author in his book entitled "Roman Catholicism in the United States"—1950 churches for 3,500,000 people, or one church for every 1700 persons, in 1870 there were over 72,000 churches for 38,000,000, or one church for every 529 persons; "so while the population increased eleven times the number of churches increased thirty-seven times;" he says with satisfaction, and Americans must admit, though with horror, that "the growth of Catholicism in the United States for the last hundred years, has been, indeed, bewildering; in 1776 there were in that country about 25,000 Catholics all told, or 1-120th part of all the inhabitants, and now there are over 7,000,000 of them, or one-seventh of the whole population."

The words of Froude should be read by those who are not afraid to risk a further experiment: "The New World was first offered to the holders of the old traditions. They were the husbandmen first chosen for the new vineyard, and blood and desolation were the only fruits which they reared upon it. In their hands it was becoming a kingdom, not of God, but of the devil, and a sentence of blight went out against them and against their works. How fatally it has worked, let modern Spain and Spanish America bear witness."

But Roman Catholicism undergoes a change on American soil, still persist those who have unlimited faith in the passive influence of American ideas; an Asiatic serpent, fostered in Indian Buddhism, the source of religious or Christian pessimism, as Oswald affirms, will have all his venom extracted, his propensity to coil and crush, by simply basking in a well-cultivated American garden or twining around its fruit-trees. But "it has long been the proud but most unholy boast of the Roman Church that she never changes," writes H. F. Barnard in the "Index," and then goes to the case in point: "Papal indulgence was the rock on which the Christian Church split three hundred and fifty years ago; yet on this same question of indulgence, Rome has not altered one jot or tittle of her pretensions," which he demonstrates by extracts from the "Messenger of St. Joseph's Union," to all the members of which Papal indulgence has been granted by Pope Leo XIII., and which advertises the sale of masses at one dollar each, thereby doing a thriving trade. A few extracts taken from the pastoral published at the fourth Provincial Council at Cincinnati, March 19th, 1882, will show in how far the Romish Church has changed its tenets or adopted American habits of thought. "A systematic and combined effort, both in Europe and America, is being made to secularize religion, and to substitute for God and religion science and material progress. It is claimed that all men are 'free and equal,' and under that cry religion and law are assailed. . . . Nor are all men equal. . . . This is in the nature of things and must be, as it is ordained by God that some shall rule and some shall be ruled. Those who are appointed to rule have certain rights that subjects have not. Hence kings and magistrates, and bishops and priests, are appointed to rule; if to rule, then they are above those whom they rule. . . . With the popular doctrine that all men are equal, there is steadily growing the doctrine that 'all power is from the people,' and that they who exercise authority in the state do not exercise it as their own, but as intrusted to them by the people, and upon this condition—that it may be recalled by the will of the same people by whom it was confided to them. This is not Catholic doctrine, nor is it the doctrine of the Scriptures, which teach: 'By me kings reign . . . by me princes rule, and the mighty decree justice.' 'Give ear, you that rule the people, . . . for power is given to you by God, and strength by the Most High.' 'Let every soul be subject to the higher powers, for there is no power but from God; and those that are, are ordained of God.' . . . There is also a growing disposition among a class of Catholics to teach that in some things the priest receives his power from the people. There is also a disposition to draw lines and to confine the priest within limits that neither God nor religion can permit. The priest is not appointed by the people, nor does he receive his power from the people. He receives his power from God, and the people are commanded to seek the law from his lips, 'for the priest's lips should keep knowledge.'

'He that hears you hears me,' says Christ, speaking of His priests, 'and he that despises you despises me.' 'Go teach' are words that leave no doubt as to the right of priests to teach, or the duty of the people to listen. . . . Governments and States and peoples are alike subject to the law of God equally as the humblest. Governments have no more right to do wrong than individuals. 'All power comes from God,' and the Church is the witness and guardian of revelation, as well as the interpreter thereof. From her the world must learn the law of God, and the law of man must ever be subordinated to the law of God. It is untrue to assert that 'all power comes from the people.' 'All power comes from God,' by whom princes rule, and the mighty decree justice."

It will not do to leave these tedious injunctions that have been reiterated since the second century, unchanged and unamended, without including those relative to the school-question, the most serious annoyance the Roman Catholics have to contend with in the United States: "Religion must form a part of the education of the child. Education without religion may have the glitter of science, but it will not have the essence of virtue. Virtue must be the foundation of education, but religion is the foundation of virtue; hence we hold religion must form a part of the daily education of the child, and must be taught co-ordinately with science and the cognate branches. Deeply impressed with the necessity of training Catholic children in the faith of their fathers, whilst waiting a change in the public-school system, in which our just rights as citizens shall be recognized and conceded, there remains to us but to appeal to the generosity of our ever faithful people to continue to support our Catholic schools. We know too well how heavy the burden is, and how unjust it is that Catholics are forced to support their own schools and at the same time be taxed to support a public-school system from which, for conscience sake, they can receive no benefit. Wherever, therefore, throughout the province, Catholic schools are not yet established, pastors will use all diligence that they be established, being ever mindful of the instructions sent by the Holy See to the American bishops to see that Catholic schools be everywhere established, and that in them not only science and profane knowledge be taught, but also religion, the queen of all sciences. It is, therefore, our wish, that the church and school go hand in hand; that where the one is, there also shall the other be."

The tendency of all this is as plain as its meaning. There is the denial that the principles embodied in the American Constitution are right; the people are *not* free and equal; power is *not* from the people; there should *not* be self-rule, but "kings and magistrates, and bishops and priests are appointed to rule;" secular government and secular education are utterly obnoxious to the Romish Church, and it is bound by all the laws of its own organization to eradicate them. The members of this Church are consequently the only class of emigrants to the United States who are not loyal to the institutions of the country they live in, who do not in any sense assimilate with the principles of these institutions; under the guise of American citizens they are actually traitors, only waiting for the moment when they can deal a death-blow to the government and rulers their mediæval superstition has taught them to abhor. Their arrogance inflated and buoyed up by the remembrance of the historical fact that the power to which alone they yield allegiance was able to destroy the civilization of ancient Greece, that of the Moors, to sap the strength of Scandinavia and cause its decline, to reduce all Europe to a state of misery and barbarism that lasted for a thousand years, they regard the repetition of this atrocious work in the United States as an easy task, and set about it years ago with the confidence and precision that distinguished their European efforts. Conscious as Americans are of their own strength, the power of their own nation, they should not underestimate the strength of their insidious foe, nor forget that this foe vanquished the Greeks, the Saxons, the Moors, the Albigenses, the French Protestants, the Scandinavians, getting the better through their craft and hellish devices—never through legitimate or honest means—of whole communities and nations who cherished advanced thoughts, republican principles, who were free-minded, enlightened and cultivated. The history of Europe does not show an even and harmonious development, Christianity or Romanism succeeding a state of greater barbarism and gradually ameliorating human conditions, but a violent substitution of barbarism for the civilization and enlightenment it ruthlessly quenched. All of these highly civilized races struggled manfully for their existence, and in the case of the Scandinavians, offered five hundred years of determined opposition to the demoniac legions of the Church; but Americans make no resistance whatsoever; they even praise the vampyre that has fastened upon them, as manifest from an editorial in the "Boston Transcript," headed "A Boston Cardinal," in which these words appear: "None the less should our fathers, brought up as they had been to abominate the Scarlet Woman, be credited with tolerance in aiding the little flock of Catholics to find shelter and comfort and to wax strong. The history of the Church in this city is one of the most interesting chapters in our annals. It is interesting, not only as all religious experiences must be to all thinking men, but as showing a great social change which has been working on our people. The Roman Catholic Church to-day is great, powerful, flourishing, and perfectly organized in our midst, and yet it is but little over eighty years since the old cathedral was dedicated, and it is but seventy-five since the first Bishop of Boston received his consecration."

In the nature of things the Romish power will work thus quietly and peaceably only for a limited space of time. The period of gentle and persuasive measures has obviously been protracted in the United States by reason of the unprecedented success that attended the manœuvres of the Mother Church, so strangely facilitated by the unsuspecting attitude of Americans. Were they *really* so republican-minded, when they thus permitted the advance of the most monarchical of dominions ? But Mr. Gladstone, in his " Rome and the Newest Fashions in Religion," draws attention to the fact that another policy, the one that has proved so efficacious heretofore, is contemplated, in Europe, if not in America : " My propositions then, as they stood, are these :

"1. That Rome has substituted for the proud boast of *semper eadem*, a policy of violence and change in faith.

" 2. That she has refurbished and paraded anew every rusty tool she was fondly thought to have disused.

" 3. That no one can now become her convert without renouncing his moral and mental freedom, and placing his civil loyalty and duty at the mercy of another.

" 4. That she (Rome) has equally repudiated modern thought and ancient history."

Furthermore he says : " It leads many to the painful and revolting conclusion that there is a fixed purpose among the secret inspirers of Roman policy to pursue, by the road of force, upon the arrival of any favourable opportunity, the favourite project of re-erecting the terrestrial throne of the Popedom, even if it can only be re-erected on the ashes of the city and amidst the whitening bones of the people." In confirmation of this horrible probability, the author cites the words of Cardinal Manning, in which the intention stands plainly revealed, at the League of St. Sebastian, on the 20th of January, 1874 : " Now, when the nations of Europe have revolted, and when they have dethroned, as far as men can dethrone, the Vicar of Jesus Christ, and when they have made the usurpation of the Holy City a part of international law—when all this has been done, there is only one solution of the difficulty—a solution, I fear, impending —and that is the terrible scourge of continental war : a war, which will exceed the horrors of any of the wars of the first empire. I do not see how this can be averted. And it is my firm conviction, that, in spite of all obstacles, the Vicar of Jesus Christ will be put again in his own rightful place." Nor is this all. "The Catholic Church," he says, "cannot be silent, it cannot hold its peace; it cannot cease to preach the doctrines of Revelation, not only of the Trinity and of the Incarnation, but likewise of the Seven Sacraments, and of the Infallibility of the Church of God, and of the necessity of Unity, and of the Sovereignty, both spiritual and temporal, of the Holy See."

There is still another threat, couched in the following words: "If Christian princes and their laws deviate from the law of God, the Church has authority from God to judge of that deviation, and *by all its powers* to enforce the correction of that departure from justice."

It is more than apparent that the sins of the American Republic must far outweigh those of any Christian prince in Europe; there is not a point in which the Republican and the Roman Catholic code coincide; what then is the retribution that the Holy See will mete out to Americans, when the time comes? And why is the hour of retribution delayed?

Coming events hinge on the stand taken by the United States on the Columbus question. J. J. Barry may be considered to interpret literally the views of his Church when he says that "the first object of the Discovery, disengaged from every human consideration, was, therefore, the glorification of the Redeemer and the extension of His Church." I have quoted these words before, but they cannot be too forcibly impressed upon the mind. The object was not impeded by any uncertainty with regard to the discovery, for it was not to be a *discovery*, it was simply to be the claiming of lands before discovered and to which the route had been marked out. The Church as usual had chosen an infallible method. It leaves experimenting to scientists. Washington Irving describes the precipitate haste with which Pope and sovereigns took possession of the new territory, predestined for Papal rule: "In the midst of their rejoicings, the Spanish sovereigns lost no time in taking every measure necessary to secure their new acquisitions . . . took the immediate precaution to secure the sanction of the Pope (Alexander VI.) . . a pontiff whom some historians have stigmatized with every vice and crime that could disgrace humanity." The records of his crimes are too revolting to read; debauchery, incest, murder, robbery, and assassination for the end of robbery, distinguish this monster's life, until by drinking, by mistake, some of the poisoned wine intended for nine wealthy cardinals and some other opulent persons whom he had invited to a banquet, the career of the infamous wretch was closed. "The present discovery," continues Irving, "was a still greater achievement" (than the conquest of Granada); "it was the fulfilment of one of the sublime promises to the Church; it was giving to it the heathen for an inheritance and the uttermost parts of the earth for a possession." A Bull was issued, dated May 2nd, 1493, "ceding to the Spanish sovereigns the same rights, privileges, and indulgences in respect to the newly discovered region, as had been accorded to the Portuguese, with regard to their African discoveries, under the same condition of planting and propagating the Catholic faith."

s the American Republic disposed to consider itself tributary to Spain and to allow these Spanish plans to be carried out to the letter? If so, it has but to accept the Spanish and Roman Catholic version of the discovery and suffer these schemes to blot out the Norse discovery of America. It must then endow Columbus with all his prerogatives, saintship included, and worship his memory. It would be such a glorious thing for the United States to be under the charge of a tutelar saint, to have its St. Christopher, as Norway had its St. Olaf and Sweden its St. Birgitta, after they became Christianized or *Romanized!*

But as this response to Spanish demands does not lie within the range of human probability, what is the alternative? To

D

proclaim the fact of the Norse discovery and denounce the Columbian one as a deliberate fraud of the Church, devised for proselyting purposes. The true tendency of America was given when the Norsemen landed on its shores; it was a good augury for the future nation, for these were brave, free, high-minded men, men of a race who had planted the seeds of liberty in many a state of Europe, and who did it in this case unwittingly, from the mere force of their splendid nationality.

Columbus, the bigoted Roman Catholic adventurer, who fed his ambition and greed on the narratives of the Norse voyages to America, read secretly in Iceland, strove to give the New World the opposite tendency, the downward tendency. Which shall prevail?

CHAPTER II.

THE MANIFEST DUTY OF THE UNITED STATES IN THIS QUESTION.

THAT deeply interesting work by William and Mary Howitt, "The History and Romance of Northern Europe," opens with an exclamation, an indignant one: "Amongst the many wonders of this world, there is none greater than the blindness of the writers of this and other countries to the transcendent influence of the blood and spirit of ancient Scandinavia on the English character." In reading up on this subject, Mallet's "Northern Antiquities" is one of the first books likely to fall into one's hands—a pioneer work in itself—and this paragraph but increases the amazement: "History has not recorded the annals of a people who have occasioned greater, more sudden, or more numerous revolutions in Europe than the Scandinavians, or whose antiquities, at the same time, are so little known."

So little known! How is that? The Scandinavians have themselves formed the early history of nearly every nation in Europe, of France, Switzerland, Russia, England, Scotland, besides forming the entire history of their own countries,—how can one study English history, without learning all about these people, or French history, without the same result, or Scotch, or Swiss, or Russian? Were their achievements really so great, as the world takes so little note of them? One reads a little farther in this French work, which Bishop Percy was enterprising enough to put into English in 1847, and strikes upon the following passage: "It is easy to see from this short sketch, how greatly the nations of the North have influenced the different fates of Europe ; and if it be worth while to trace its revolutions to their causes, if the illustration of its institutions, of its police, of its customs, of its manners, of its laws, be a subject of useful and interesting inquiry ; it must be allowed, that the antiquities of the North, that is to say, everything which tends to make us acquainted with its ancient inhabitants, merits a share in the attention of thinking men. But to render this obvious by a particular example ; is it not well known that the most flourishing and celebrated states of Europe owe originally to the Northern nations, whatever liberty they now enjoy, either in their constitution, or in the spirit of their government ? "

Such a race so little known ? There must be some mystery under this ! What do English authors say about it ? How do they account for it ? Grenville Pigott, in his " Scandinavian Mythology," says this : " The omission of any serious research into the religion of Odin, by men of such profound learning, as was possessed by many of our early antiquarians, may, not unnaturally, raise a doubt in the minds of some of the degree of advantage or interest likely to result from an inquiry of this nature ; but a brief account of the circumstances which attended the overthrow of heathenism and the introduction of Christianity in those countries, where the Scandinavian deities were chiefly worshipped, may otherwise explain the cause of this silence on a subject so likely to have invited earnest inquiry."

This gives one an inkling of the cause, to be sure, but yet it remains an incomprehensible enigma how the history of the most remarkable race that ever trod the earth could have been thus buried in oblivion ! And that the English people know nothing about them, know nothing about their own ancestors, that is the strangest part of it ! But perhaps it is a mistake, the neglect of this subject ascribed to Great Britain as well as France, only a casual remark by one or two authors not cognizant themselves of the extent of English or French research. Let us look further; Henry Wheaton, in his "History of the Northmen, or Danes and Normans from the Earliest Times to the Conquest of England by William of Normandy," makes the same comment: "In the following attempt to illustrate the early annals of the North, it has been the writer's aim to seize the principal points in the progress of society and manners in this remote period, which have been either entirely passed over, or barely glanced at by the national historians of France and England, but which throw a strong and clear light upon the affairs of Europe during the middle ages, and illustrate the formation of the great monarchies now constituting some of its leading states." Samuel Laing says: "The social condition, institutions, laws and literature of this vigorous, influential branch of the race, have been too much overlooked by our historians and political philosophers." In the preface to his translation of the "Heimskringla" he gravely reveals his intention of stepping in and repairing the serious omission of these historians and philosophers, of averting the consequences of their intentional neglect of certain phases and racial characteristics, the concomitants of early English history, without which there can be no intelligent reading of that history, and to do this he imposes upon himself the double work of clothing in English dress the noble work by Snorre Sturleson, an historian, who, in his turn, has done for England what England has failed to do for itself, by writing his "Chronicle of the Kings of Norway," kings, many of them, who played an important rôle in England and Scotland,—and of composing the preliminary dissertation, a perusal of which comprises a thorough course of instruction for the reader in this almost unknown subject. The Rev. Edmund F. Slafter, who edited Beamish's translation of "The Voyages of the Northmen to America," pays this earnest and enthusiastic author a just tribute when he says : "Mr. Laing's dissertation is a thorough discussion of the whole subject of Northern literature and history, and is rendered not the less interesting by the frank and bold manner in which the author expresses his opinions on some important questions." The words in the preface are these: " It is of importance to English history to have, in the English language, the means of judging of the social and intellectual state—of the institutions and literature—of a people who during three hundred years bore an important, and for a great portion of that time a predominant part, not merely in the wars, but in the legislation of England; who occupied a very large portion of the country, and were settled in its best lands in such numbers as to be governed by their own, not by Anglo-Saxon laws; and who undoubtedly must be the forefathers of as large a proportion of the present English nation as the Anglo-Saxons themselves, and of a much larger proportion than the Normans. These Northmen have not merely been the forefathers of the people, but of the institutions and character of the nation, to an extent not sufficiently considered by our historians. . . . They occupied one-third of all England for many generations, under their own Danish laws; and for half a century nearly, immediately previous to the Norman Conquest, they held the supreme government of the country." Was the supremacy of these Northern people such a disgrace to England that the proud nation has not yet recovered from the humiliation of it, and cannot endure to be reminded of those times? Manifestly not. Did these Scandinavians so retard the progress of the nation that the people of modern England may justly hate them for the injury and banish them, so far as may be, from recollection? Every line of evidence refutes such an idea. But aside from the military prowess and warlike achievements of this race, which all must admit, did they have any prestige that entitles them to a place in English literature, in English history, in the grateful memory of the nation? In his words with regard to Snorre Sturleson and the subject-matter of his remarkable book, Laing settles the question as to the right of this race to a place in English literature and history : " He gives, too, every now and then, very natural touches of character, and scenes of human action, and of the working of the human mind, which are in truth highly dramatic. In rapid narrative of the stirring events of the wild Viking life,—of its vicissitudes, adventures and exploits,—in extraordinary, yet not improbable incidents and changes in the career of individuals,—in touches true to nature,—and in the admirable management of his story, in which episodes apparently the most unconnected with his subject, come in by and by at the right moment, as most essential parts of it,—Snorre Sturleson stands as far above Ville Hardouin, Joinville or Froissart, as they stand above the monkish chroniclers who preceded them. His true seat in the Valhalla of European literature is on the same bench—however great the distance between—on the same bench with Shakspeare, Carlyle, and Scott, as a dramatic historian; for his Harold Haarfager, his Olaf Tryggvason, his Olaf the Saint, are in reality great historical dramas, in which these wild, energetic personages, their adherents and their opponents, are presented working, acting and speaking before you. . . . English readers . . . who would never discover from the pages of Hume, or of any other of our historical writers, that the Northern pagans who, in the ninth and tenth centuries, ravaged the coasts of Europe, sparing neither age, sex nor condition—respecting neither churches, monasteries nor their inmates—conquering Normandy, Northumberland (then reckoned with East Anglia, equal to one-third of all England), and, under Swein and Canute the Great, conquering and ruling over the whole of England,—were a people possessing any literature at all, or any laws, institutions, arts, or manners connecting them with civilized life. Our historians have confined themselves for information entirely to the records and chronicles of the Anglo-Saxon monks . . . and who naturally represent them as the most ferocious and ignorant of barbarians, and without any tincture of civilization."

There we have it; the monks, the natural enemies of the Scandinavians, have become their historians, and the testimony of those whose whole office has been to propagate such versions only of facts and events and personal action as pass Church censorship, has been universally accepted. Hume does indeed imitate the tone of these monks, whose rage will never cool toward the Northmen, for he uniformly speaks of them as "those swarms of robbers, which the fertile North thus incessantly poured forth against them," "the piratical Danes," "those ravagers," &c., &c.; and makes one representation as egregiously false as if penned under monkish dictation: "When Alfred came to the throne he found the nation sunk into the grossest ignorance and barbarism, proceeding from the continued disorders in the government, and from the ravages of the Danes. The monasteries were destroyed, the monks butchered or dispersed, their libraries burnt; and thus the only seats of erudition in those ages were totally subverted."

It will be seen further on that there was one "seat of erudition" in the world even then, that preserved the true history of those times so sacredly as to place it, intact, in the hands of posterity, for effective use in the hour when the records so skilfully manipulated by ecclesiastics and religious intriguers would be discredited and proofs of the fraud required. This true history was preserved in the heart and mind of the people of the North, ages before it was reduced to writing, and handed down in oral tradition. There was also an especial class of men to whose keeping all annals were confided, and Laing's description of them, here quoted, corresponds with that of many other writers on the subject: "Before the introduction or general diffusion of writing, it is evident that a class of men whose sole occupation was to commit to memory and preserve the laws, usages, precedents and details of all those civil affairs and rights, and to whose fidelity in relating former transactions implicit confidence could be given, must of necessity have existed in society—must have been in every locality; and from the vast number and variety of details in every district, and the great interests of every community, must have been esteemed and recompensed in proportion to their importance in such a social state. This class were the Skalds."

This paragraph, in itself, contradicts the following one by Hume: "He (Rollo) collected a body of troops, which like that of all those ravagers, was composed of Norwegians, Swedes, Frisians, Danes, and adventurers of all nations, who being accustomed to a roving, unsettled life, took delight in nothing but war and plunder." As well could one say of the French followers of Napoleon who accompanied him on his wars of conquest, that "they were accustomed to a roving, unsettled life." This same Rollo, or Rolf, achieved a conquest in France, that Napoleon himself need not have been ashamed of, and which perhaps conduced to make the French people worthy followers of the great general, who may have been inspired to heroic efforts by the accounts of his illustrious predecessor, William the Conqueror. Rolf left Norway for the same reason as did "the nobility and people of the highest civilization" who emigrated to Iceland, namely, to escape from the despotic sway of Harald Hårfager, and neither he and his followers nor they were men to "take delight in nothing but war and plunder."

On the accuracy of the old Icelandic annals must the thinkers and reformers of the present day rely, in their efforts to disentangle history from the almost hopeless confusion in which the aforesaid monkish chroniclers have involved it, consequently it is extremely gratifying to find such ample corroboration of the truthfulness of the Icelandic statements. It must never be lost from sight that these were a *free* people, bound by neither priest nor king, and consequently not forced to extol the representatives of either ecclesiasticism or royalty; they expressed their honest opinion in every instance. Five hundred years of Roman Catholic rule had destroyed all manhood and independence in the Anglo-Saxons; as Laing says, "the spirit, character and national vigour of the old Anglo-Saxon branch of this people, had evidently become extinct under the influence and pressure of the Church of Rome upon the energies of the human mind." But the Scandinavians were as yet exempt; submission and all cringing to authority was unknown to them; there was no cowardice in their blood, and hence no propensity to lie. In the introduction to his Heimskringla, Snorre Sturleson, the celebrated man "to whom," as Henry Wheaton declares, "his country's history and literature are most indebted, and whose great historical work has justly earned for him the title of the Northern Herodotus," affirms with regard to the truthfulness of the Skalds: "For although it be the fashion with Scalds to praise most those in whose presence they are standing, yet no one would dare to relate to a chief what he and all those who heard it know to be false and imaginary,—not a true account of his deeds; because that would be mockery, not praise."

In the twelfth century Iceland possessed considerable collections of books, and for a long time one common language was spoken and written in England, Iceland, Norway, Sweden and Denmark. At least one-third of England was occupied by men from the North, the land was ruled by Northern laws, Northern customs and usages had been introduced. Why then have not modern English historians sought their own race, their own nationality, their own language, as the right sources of historical knowledge of England, instead of the old Latin legends which are the nonsensical relics of Roman rule in this country? To which has their allegiance been due, to which has it spontaneously been given, to the Roman rule which has left traces only of "a despotic military occupation of the country," even this soon obliterated, or to the Scandinavian rule, which has made England the proud nation that it is? There was no stint of historical records in Iceland, its literature was as rich and varied as it was copious, the Latin lore (?) of the monks could in no sense be compared with it, for, to cite Laing, "during the five centuries in which the Northmen were riding over the seas, and conquering wheresoever they landed, the literature of the people they overcame was locked up in a dead language, and within the walls of monasteries. But the Northmen had a literature of their own, rude as it was; and the Anglo-Saxon race had none, none at least belonging to the people."

One Icelandic collection, the Arnæ-Magnæan collection, "alone contains two thousand volumes of Icelandic and old Northern manuscripts. This collection was made by Arnas Magnussen, a distinguished antiquary, between 1702 and 1712, and is named in honour of him." (*Vide* the Earl of Ellesmere's "Guide to Old Northern Archæology." London, 1848, p. 128.) Did England seek to gain possession of these treasures? Evidently not, for the bulk of them found their way to *Denmark*. The Earl of Ellesmere remarks: "But it is not merely for the Scandinavian North properly so called, that the language and literature possess a national significance, which, throughout a certain period, extends to Russia, as also to Germany and to France, . . . but doubtless in a still greater degree to the British Isles." True in theory, this is disproved in practice, for the English nation has not given the slightest evidence that it considers this language and literature to possess a national significance; its learned men and antiquarians have disdained to pursue this line of research, the people, said to be most proud of their ancestry, have buried all recollection of the only ancestors of theirs of whom they had reason to be proud; a land, said to be enlightened, has purposely thrown a veil of obscurity over its own most brilliant epochs which little Denmark is obliged to lift, in order to give the world the information to which it is rightfully entitled and which it is hopeless to expect from England! English tourists go to Norway *to fish and to hunt*, not to search for historical links, nor to gain a better knowledge of their Viking ancestry; the museums and fine antiquarian collections in Denmark possess as little attractions for the cultivated travelling public of England as the historical relics and associations of Sweden. But sixty hours by sea from that country, one that would naturally be supposed to possess an infinite charm for the English, what with its lovely scenery, its castles and manors, its Viking mounds and burial-places, its exhumed treasures,—a priceless illuminated scroll of English history as well as Swedish,—the English people have too little interest to go there! In England Swedish literature, together with Norwegian and Danish, is excluded; there is a deep-seated prejudice against translations, *even from the language derived from the one that was once their own national tongue;* Swedish authors are scarcely known even by name. Sweden itself is held in downright contempt; an expression of surprise covers the listener's face if one speaks of any of the excellent features of this country, or its productions in literature or art; the same contempt would fall upon Norway but for its salmon and bears and wild mountain haunts, which afford to tired summer travellers a refuge from the *over-civilization* of England. Denmark is not taken into the account at all. With a narrow provincialism that is unparalleled, England lops off its own past, the most glorious epochs of its antiquity, forbids the mention of its Viking ancestors, is deaf to all knowledge of them, and excludes the three nations whose early history is identical with its own from all fraternity or kinship!

So the records and annals went to Denmark! To an American, the Rev. E. F. Slafter, the public is indebted for a graphic account of the use to which these valuable manuscripts were put; this is contained in his introduction to "The Voyages of the Northmen to America:" "The Royal Society of Northern Antiquaries, at Copenhagen, entered upon the investigation of the subject with enthusiasm, energy and comprehensive views. Their scheme involved a much wider field than the visits of the Northmen to America. It comprehended a thorough investigation of the whole subject of Scandinavian history and literature. The Society proposed to publish from time to time such old Northern manuscripts as might be useful in the elucidation of history, antiquities and language. The field was divided into sections; and active workers were appointed to each, selected with reference to their especial tastes and learning. The fruits of these labours were prolific; and in the progress of a few years more than forty volumes were issued, besides gazettes and annual reports, dealing with early Scandinavian life, manners and customs, in their multiform conditions and phases. In 1837, Professor Charles Christian Rafn, who had been placed at the head of the section on the voyages to America, published, under the auspices of the Society, an elaborate report, in a volume entitled 'Antiquitates Americanæ,' an imperial quarto of 526 pages, richly embellished with numerous illustrations and maps, comprising facsimilies of the most important parchment codices, which had been taken as the basis of the work. In this volume the treatment of the whole subject is thorough and scholarly. While it is never safe to assume that the treatment of any historical question is absolutely complete and exhaustive, we apprehend that little or nothing more will ever be added to our knowledge of the voyages made to this country by the Northmen in the tenth century."

Pigott also communicates some information on the subject: "In 1594 appeared a Danish translation of Snorre Sturleson's 'Chronicle of the Kings of Norway,' written in the thirteenth century in Icelandic, which threw an entirely new light on this hitherto obscure subject, and excited the further researches of the learned in the North. One of the most ardent in this pursuit was Arngrim Johnsen, who died in 1648, and who by his writings and industry in procuring and deciphering old Icelandic manuscripts, obtained a great mass of information on the subject. Contemporary with him, and his worthy co-adjutor, was Bryniulf Svendsen, Bishop of Iceland, who died in 1675. The former discovered and sent to Olaus Wormius, in 1628, a parchment copy of the Prose Edda, now in the Library of the University at Copenhagen, and scarcely ten years afterwards, Bryniulf discovered copies on parchment both of the Prose and Poetic Eddas, and sent both to the Royal Library at Copenhagen."

Not content with assuming the whole tremendous task of making this buried history known, with performing its own duty and England's, too, with informing the American nation of those facts in its own early history, long before it became a nation, which have alone saved it from impending ruin, from another " thousand years' eclipse of common sense and reason " (as Oswald describes the state in Europe incident upon the Romanizing process), Denmark proposes to do still more, this largely for the benefit of England. According to what the Earl of Ellesmere says : " It has been the wish of the Royal Society of Northern Antiquaries, when its means should admit of it, to publish a collection, as complete as possible, of the Scandinavian sources of the early history of Great Britain and Ireland, in a separate work, to form a companion to the two works already undertaken by the Society, viz. 'Antiquitates Americanæ' and 'Antiquités Russes et Orientales.' . . . The importance of a similar collection of 'Antiquitates Britannicæ et Hibernicæ' must be obvious. . . . When a greater degree of attention shall be bestowed in the British Islands on the undertakings of the Society and a greater degree of interest awakened for the matter in question, it is to be expected that the Society will thereby be enabled to realize such a plan."

So little Denmark is even to undertake the publication of English history, which England is too indifferent and inert to publish for itself! As another evidence of this wilful ignorance and disregard of a subject of such vast importance, I quote a significant little note in N. L. Beamish's book: "'Illustrations of Northern Antiquities,' 4to, Edinburgh, 1814, a work of high value and great promise, but which the want of public support compelled the distinguished compilers and antiquaries, Jamieson and Weber, to discontinue." As it is necessary to heap up evidence on this point, so that no doubt may be left of the truth in the mind of any reader, I quote some more testimony to this sad, almost inexplicable fact of England's remissness, which might have cost the United States so dearly; Mallet says: "The sources whence issued those torrents of people, which from the North overwhelmed all Europe, the principles which put them in motion, and gave them so much activity and force, these objects, so grand and interesting, have been but slightly and weakly treated of." Pigott says, and Pigott is an English writer: "It is within a comparatively recent period only, that the early history of the North of Europe has begun to attract much attention in this country. Previous to the publication of Mallet's 'Northern Antiquities' all that was known on the subject rested chiefly on meagre notices gleaned from Roman writers, whose authority on this subject, from deficiency of sources of accurate information, was, to say the least, doubtful; and on the exaggerated account of the Monkish Chroniclers, who had too good reason not to love the people whom they described. Hence the history of the Scandinavians or Northmen, as they were afterwards called, has been generally looked upon as a mere sanguinary chronicle of piracies, murders and gloomy superstitions, and but little inclination felt to explore a field so uninviting. To those, however, whose curiosity has led them to examine the copious sources of information respecting the early religion and history of Northern Europe, furnished by the Eddas and by the numerous Sagas which exist in the libraries of Copenhagen and Stockholm; it cannot fail to appear a curious anomaly that, whilst the Grecian Mythology in all its varied details is made familiar to us from our childhood, we have been so long content to remain in great measure ignorant of the religious superstitions of our immediate ancestors; superstitions inferior it may be to those of Greece in refinement, but scarcely so in wildness or sublimity; which contributed so much to form the peculiar character that still distinguishes the inhabitants of Northern Europe; which even yet linger in the traditions of our peasantry, and whose traces are enduringly marked in the names of some of our festivals, and especially of the days of our week."

He says yet more; for once on this subject any thinking and truth-loving person, who values what is best in the past, will wax earnest and indignant: "The mythology of the ancient Scandinavians, respecting which so much curious information has been brought to light, of late years, by the researches of many distinguished writers, in Germany, Denmark, and Sweden, has hitherto excited but little attention in this country, although the subject is well calculated to awaken our interest, not only as the source of most of our popular superstitions, from whence the favourite authors of our early childhood and of our maturer age have drawn their witches, their dwarves, their giants, and their ghosts, but in an historical point of view also, for a short retrospect will suffice to show that the religion of Odin must have exercised a great and lasting influence on the character and institutions of the inhabitants of Great Britain."

Not from Eddas or Sagas, nor the "Heimskringla," nor the rich stores of information put within easy reach by zealous Danish antiquarians, has England drawn the scanty knowledge that it was constrained to put into some kind of historical shape. That English historians have been obliged to consult *some* authorities, reliable or unreliable, is self-evident. The authors I have quoted are unanimous in asserting that they consulted the monkish chroniclers by preference. Having had a heroic age, this transmitted to them by the conquering hosts who settled and governed England, having gained through these people, a race combining the most superb traits, a mythology, equal if not superior to the Grecian, an ancient literature of which any land could be proud, and which was virtually the only literature in Europe at that time, having had a past to which not only England, but other nations owe all the liberty they possess, the English consult the records of a class of men whose sole office during all the ages in question was to eradicate both the Grecian and Scandinavian mythologies, to blast literature, to get the better, by fair means or foul, of the race who were sowing the seeds of liberty broad-cast over Europe, and whose sole office since that period has been to blacken the past in which the free-born Scandinavians figured and to so defame them that posterity would regard them as monsters!

Laing is able to say who and what some of these men were personally: "Our early historians, from the venerable Bede downwards, however accurate in the events and dates they record, and however valuable for this accuracy, are undeniably the dullest of chroniclers. They were monks, ignorant of the world beyond their convent-walls, recording the death of their abbots, the legends of their founders, and the miracles of their sainted brethren, as the most important events in history; the facts being stated without exercise of judgment, or inquiry after truth, the fictions with a dull credulity unenlivened by a single gleam of genius. . . . It is not to be denied that all this connected series of Anglo-Saxon and Anglo-Norman history, from the dissolution of the Roman empire in Britain in the middle of the fifth century down to the middle of the thirteenth century, although composed by such writers of the Anglo-Saxon population as Bede and Matthew Paris, men the most eminent of their times for learning and literary attainments amongst the Anglo-Saxons and their descendants, is of the most unmitigated dullness, considered as literary or intellectual production; and that all the historical compositions of the old Anglo-Saxon branch during those eight centuries, either in England or in Germany, are, with few if any exceptions, of the same leaden character."

These in England and France, distorting the characteristics of the Norsemen and Vikings, and concealing everything that was to their credit, and the monkish writers in Spain and Italy extolling Columbus a few centuries later, a man after their own heart, *both* sedulously hiding the fact of the Norse discovery of America, which the Romish Church must of necessity have known at the date of its accomplishment, all these conspired to prepare a pitfall for the future American Republic, which it will be barely able to escape.

English predilections were obviously with the monks, with the Church; not only did the English people accept and disseminate the garbled versions of these professional falsifiers relative to the deeds of their own ancestors and kinsmen, but they joined forces with them to subdue the nations of the North through the only means available—that is by converting them to Christianity. This was their last resort, a stratagem of war of those deficient in genuine military qualifications, and who could not overcome their enemy by legitimate means. English missionaries and priests went to Norway, Sweden, and Denmark, and laboured indefatigably to convert the inhabitants. "It was from *England*," affirms the Earl of Ellesmere proudly, "that Norway received the first germ of Christianity. It was *there* that Hakon, the first Christian king of Norway, commenced and finished his education, during the period from 937 to 963, though he failed in the effort to establish his own faith among his subjects. . . . It was reserved for the insignificant islets of Scilly to kindle for Norway that light, which was thence to be diffused over the remotest North. The expatriated Norwegian prince and sea-king, Olaf Tryggvason, known in the history of England by the name of Anlaf, received baptism in these isles in 993."

It is well known what atrocities Olaf Tryggvason perpetrated in forcing his subjects to adopt Christianity. English bishops also converted Olaf Ericson, king of Sweden, in 1008. Wheaton has something significant to relate about the Hakon referred to: Harald Hårfager's son, Hakon, who had been educated in the new religion at the court of King Athelstane, took with him from England some Christian priests and missionaries. He assembled a large conclave of people, where he tried to introduce this doctrine. A rich and popular landholder rose to oppose it, and made a fervent protest, in which he said: "But now we know not what to think, that thou who didst restore to us our lost freedom, shouldst desire to fasten upon us a new and more intolerable yoke of slavery." Wheaton gives us the whole speech, and a remarkable oratorical effort it is! The distinguished Swedish novelist, Victor Rydberg, in "The Last Athenian," puts into the mouth of one of his anti Christian characters a similar objection: "The Christians, Hermione, hate the high expression of art, as much as the deep seriousness of investigation. They talk of poverty and plunder our temples —of humility and trample upon our necks. . . . They are a pack of malefactors, intriguers, hypocrites and asses. They tear in pieces the world and each other in disputes on words without meaning; but that in which they all agree, is what I most despise; all banish the freedom of reason, all teach that the power of rulers and the slavery of the people is from God. Freedom has departed from real life, but these people deny it even in thought."

The only way of depriving the formidable Northern lion of teeth and claws was to Christianize it. Freedom, freedom of life and action, freedom of thought, freedom in a vigour and exuberance of development never attained before, had made the Northern race dangerous, nay, absolutely fatal to the priest-ridden, enslaved masses of southern and middle Europe. The mere sight or knowledge of these grovelling, craven, black-gowned, canting hordes, inflamed the Viking rage to frenzy, inciting the utmost ferocity; it was not honourable warfare between equals, between men and men, but assault made by free, high-spirited, valiant men upon slaves, upon those whom they could not but consider their inferiors, and whom they deemed it meritorious to exterminate. The rage of the Northmen was the unconscious fury of nature against the destroyers of nature, the antipathy of health toward disease, the effort of nature to free itself from that which is inimical to it. With the instinct of self-preservation which evil has in common with good, and with the burning desire for temporal supremacy over the whole world which has ever been its animating motive, the Romish power devised and used the only possible means of rendering the Northern destroyer harmless. Subdue these hosts by force of arms it could not. Strategy and priestly craft would avail where manly courage was not at command. It was not the good of their souls nor their eternal welfare, not the inculcation of divine truth that was aimed at, but the eradication of that principle and love of freedom that rendered all of Northern blood dangerous to the Church, whose sole mission was to compel subjection to its own baleful rule. This detestation of all things Scandinavian the Romans and the Romish Church were able to instil into the English, and the two worked in concert to enslave the people of the North.

And how did they accomplish it? In the words of Wheaton: "Under the impulse of this blind zeal, Olaf Tryggvason joined treachery to cruelty as one of the means of propagating the true faith." In the "Heimskringla" we are told that "Olaf Tryggvason's short reign was in fact entirely devoted to the propagation of the new faith, by means the most revolting to humanity," and the sagas abound in instances of the exercise of the blackest deeds of darkness in spreading the light of Christianity. Many streams of noble Northern blood went to swell the tide that had been shed throughout Europe, to kill that pernicious germ of freedom that could only be destroyed through wholesale slaughter. In "The History of Rationalism," Lecky affirms: "That the Church of Rome has shed more innocent blood than any other institution that has ever existed among mankind, will be questioned by no Protestant who has a complete knowledge of history."

Among the measures used were also such as these: "Otho III., of the Saxon line, concluded a peace with Harold Blaatand, the principal condition of which was that the Danish people should embrace Christianity, and their king should endeavour to introduce the new religion in Norway." Wheaton quotes Charles the Simple's words, which so well show the disgraceful means employed: "My kingdom is laid waste," said the monarch to the prelate, "my subjects are destroyed or driven into exile; the fields are no longer ploughed or sown. Tell the Norman that I am well disposed to make a lasting peace with him, and that if he will become a Christian, I will give him broad lands and rich presents." Rolf readily consented to the proposal, as did many other leaders and generals to similar ones. There appeared to them no reason why they should not accept advantageous terms from a vanquished foe, and as for embracing Christianity, that seemed the idlest and emptiest of ceremonies to men whose religion sat so lightly upon them. To them belief in the gods was more a matter of poetry and ideality than of practical import; it served to kindle their enthusiasm, perhaps their valour, although this in the main was self-fed; and with a religion that had no rites or ceremonies to speak of, no established priesthood, that exercised no tyranny over them, it was a moral impossibility for them to conceive of such a system as the Christian Church, or to imagine to what a horrible thraldom they were consigning themselves and their descendants.

However, the mistake they made, and through no fault of

theirs either—they were too noble, too frank, too single-minded to fathom the depth of perfidy in the Romish Church, in the religious system called Christianity—this mistake the people of the United States can retrieve. The spirit of the Norsemen has descended into Americans. They, and not the English, as events have proven, are the true heirs of the glorious heritage bequeathed by the ancient Scandinavians. The colonists, who revolted against English oppression, and who threw off all allegiance to the Crown, were totally unaware that there was that in the English past that had nourished and inspired their own spirit of independence, that they had ancestors who had possessed their own distinguishing traits, and who had laboured manfully to make these traits the prevailing ones in English character, and so they cut all the links that had bound them to England.

If England had revered its own free-minded ancestors, if it had seconded the efforts of the North to spread liberty over all the nations of the earth, instead of the efforts of Rome to stifle liberty for ever by putting all nations, the Scandinavian included, under the perpetual rule of the Church, the conduct of America since the hour it became an independent Republic would have been very different and the present peril would have been averted. Precautions could then have been taken in time against the continual encroachments of the Roman Catholic power in the United States; the full purpose and design of that power would have been apparent; Americans, in a body, would have realized that while they were working, with one heart and one soul, for the formation of an ideal Republic, in which the principles of liberty, of right, of equity, of justice, would be fully embodied, there was an insidious force in their midst steadily using liberty to undermine liberty, a force that was pledged to tyranny, evil, and the subversion of right; whose record was iniquity, and whose intent was iniquity! No warning came through the watchful care of the Mother country;

it only gave the precedent of the frequent conversion of high persons from among the nobility to the Roman Catholic faith. No admonition was uttered by England to the less experienced sons and daughters of England across the water to the effect that "eternal vigilance was the price of safety." They were never told by England that they should honour their Norse ancestors, be true to the principles these held so dear, and perfect the Republic founded on a model that the Norsemen themselves had originated and outwrought in Iceland and Switzerland. The knowledge of the Norse discovery of America did not come to the people of the United States from England, but from Denmark. England took no interest in the matter, was indifferent as to whether it was true or false, felt no pride in a discovery so momentous, made by its own ancestors, saw no necessity of informing Americans of a fact of such vital importance as to prove their greatest safeguard against a deadly foe!

But Denmark came to the rescue! Denmark performed the whole duty that England had evaded. The tidings so fraught with mighty consequences to the young Republic, were seized with avidity by Americans, and responded to in the right spirit. No sooner was that great work of Professor Rafn's printed, than the Historical Society of Rhode Island opened correspondence with the Royal Society of Northern Antiquaries in Copenhagen, and several translations of the Norse voyages to America were put within reach of American readers. The Prince Society, in Boston, republished the translation of these by N. L. Beamish, an English author, who, like Laing, Pigott, the Howitts, and others, exerted himself to the utmost to rouse the English public into some sort of action, and numerous American works appeared on the subject. Gratitude was not wanting either to our Norse ancestors; the appreciation so long deferred, the tribute refused them by their English descendants, was yielded gladly by their American ones! Benjamin Lossing wrote: "It is back to the Northern Vikings we must look for the hardiest elements of progress in the United States." And B. F. De Costa: "We fable in a great measure when we speak of our Saxon inheritance; it is rather from the Northmen that we have derived our vital energy, our freedom of thought, and, in a measure that we do not yet suspect, our strength of speech." The accounts of the Norse voyages to America also seem to have met with full credence, Bancroft, the historian, forming the signal exception to the rule. Remarking this, Mr. Slafter, in his introduction to the "Voyages," says: "Mr. Bancroft, in the earliest of his "History of the United States," treats the alleged Icelandic voyages to this continent as a myth, and, in his last, has not in any degree modified his sweeping statements of distrust. We are not aware that any other distinguished historian has reached the same conclusion." Mr. Slafter himself asserts: "Both of these documents are declared, by those qualified to judge of the character of ancient writings, to be authentic, and were clearly regarded by their writers as narratives of historical truth." Edward Everett writes, quite as emphatically, in the *North American Review:* "These accounts are either founded on truth, or they are wholly false; and those who hold to the latter opinion will, we think, find more difficulty in carrying out their hypothesis, than there is in admitting the substantial truth of the tradition." Ben. Franklin, Baldwin, Goodrich, T. W. Higgenson, J. Abbott, W. C. Bryant, and many other Americans have written in confirmation of the truth of the Norse discovery of America, as founded on the Icelandic narratives.

But the duty of Americans does not end with this acknowledgment of the truth. The Roman Catholics in their midst and in Europe have been diligently spreading a statement in direct refutation of all this, the consummation of their long-continued policy of at once concealing the discovery of the Norsemen and substituting that of Columbus for it. Their gain, should this substitution be allowed, need not be described; it is already apparent enough. The wish expressed for a general celebration of the discovery of America by Columbus, is the first wary move of the Roman Catholic Church to uproot freedom from American soil. It is the signal for the renewal of the old conflict with the Norsemen in nearly every country of Europe. Once the Norse discovery is thoroughly accredited, the United States, as a nation acting upon it, the true discoverers honoured, the false one execrated as he deserves, the Church that has aided and abetted him execrated as it deserves, the kinship and sympathy of Norsemen and Americans realized and acknowledged—once this comes about, the Romish band of conspirators from Pope to canting, whining priest, have their old enemy bodily before them again, only refreshed by their long sleep of a thousand years and eager to take up the old battle on soil that will not betray them as did Europe!

Americans are to put on the Norse armour and seal the glorious work for universal liberty that their ancestors have bequeathed to them!

CHAPTER III.

THE EVIDENCE THAT THE NORSEMEN DISCOVERED AMERICA IN THE TENTH CENTURY.

As has been seen by the statement of Samuel Laing quoted in the first chapter, the proof that the Norsemen discovered America, five hundred years before Columbus, rests entirely on documentary evidence, and this evidence is to be found in the two sagas contained in the "Codex Flatoiensis." Mr. Slafter's statement is substantially the same, as far as the manuscripts are concerned: "Among the vast number of Scandinavian manuscripts there are two historical sagas which describe western voyages, undertaken during the twenty-five years that intervened between 985 and 1011. One of them is known as the Saga of Erik the Red and the other as that of Thorfinn Karlsefne. On these two documents rests all the essential evidence which we have relating to the voyages of the Northmen to America. Allusions are found in several other Scandinavian writings, which may corroborate and confirm the narratives of the two important sagas to which we have just referred, but add nothing to them really essential or important. The Saga of Erik the Red is taken from the Codex Flateyensis, containing a number of sagas, which were collected and written out in their present form at some time between the years 1387 and 1395. The original saga, of which this is a copy, is not known to be now in existence, but is conjectured, from internal evidence drawn from its language and style, to have been originally composed in the twelfth century. The saga of Thorfinn Karlsefne in its present

GULLFOSS, NEAR THE GEYSER.

Page 65.

form is supposed to have been written, at least a part of it, by Hauk Erlendson, for many years governor of Iceland, who died in 1334. Whether it had been committed to writing at an earlier period, and copied by him from a manuscript, or whether he took the narrative from oral tradition and reduced it himself to writing for the first time, is not known." In the translation of the voyages, a little light is thrown upon this point, for it is stated that "Karlsefne has accurately related to all men the occurrences on all these voyages, of which somewhat is now recited here."

But to give Mr. Slafter's full opinion concerning their reliability: "While there is no corroborating evidence outside of Icelandic writings themselves, no monuments in this country confirming the truthfulness of the narratives, they have nevertheless all the elements of truth contained in other sagas, which are clearly confirmed by monumental remains. Events occurring in Greenland, recorded in Icelandic sagas of equal antiquity, are established by the undoubted testimony of ancient monuments. This, together with the fact that there is no improbability that such voyages should have been made, render it easy to believe that the narratives contained in the sagas are true in their general outlines and important features."

The proof thus being in such a compact shape, and authentic, it only remains for us to see how this has been regarded by minds whose conclusions are of value. Among these Baron von Humboldt must naturally take precedence. Before presenting his testimony, which would have great weight, even if unsupported by that of scores of other writers, I cite Mr. Slafter's words about this testimony: "In treating of the discovery of America the author (Alex. von Humboldt) refers to the voyages of the Northmen to this continent as a matter of settled history. He does not even offer an apology, or suggest a doubt. The vast learning, just discrimination, and sound sense of this distinguished scholar, give great weight to his opinions on any subject."

The following extract is taken from the second volume of the "Cosmos:" "Although the acquaintance of the nations of Europe with the western part of the earth is the main subject of our consideration in this section, and that around which the numerous relations of a more correct and a grander view of the universe are grouped, we must yet draw a strong line of separation between the undoubted first discovery of America, in its northern portions, by the Northmen, and its subsequent re-discovery in its tropical regions. Whilst the Caliphate still flourished under the Abassides at Bagdad, and Persia was under the dominion of the Samanides, whose age was so favourable to poetry, America was discovered in the year 1000 by Leif, the son of Eric the Red, by the northern route, and as far as 41° 30' north latitude." In a foot note, the author says: "Parts of America were seen, although no landing was made on them, fourteen years before Leif Eiricksson, in the voyage which Bjarne Herjulfsson undertook from Greenland toward the southward in 986. Leif first saw the land at the island of Nantucket, 1° south of Boston; then in Nova Scotia; and, lastly, in Newfoundland, which was subsequently called 'Litla Helluland,' but never 'Vinland.' The gulf which divides Newfoundland from the mouth of the great river St. Lawrence, was called by the Northmen, who had settled in Iceland and Greenland, Markland's Gulf." (See Caroli Christiani Rafn Antiquitates Americanæ, 1845, pp. 4, 421, 423 and 463.) Baron von Humboldt thus cites the same authority, the sole and incontrovertible one. He continues: "The first, although accidental incitement towards this event emanated from Norway. Towards the close of the ninth century Naddod was driven by storms to Iceland whilst attempting to reach the Färoe Islands, which had already been visited by the Irish. The first settlement of the Northmen was made in 875 by Ingolf. Greenland, the eastern peninsula of a land which appears to be everywhere separated by the sea from America proper, was early seen" (quotes Rafn again), "although it was first peopled from Iceland a hundred years later (983). . . Notwithstanding the proximity of the opposite shores of Labrador (*Helluland it mikla*), 125 years elapsed from the first settlement of the Northmen in Iceland to Leif's great discovery of America. So small were the means possessed by a noble, enterprising, but not wealthy race for furthering navigation in these remote and dreary regions of the earth. The littoral tracts of Vinland, so called by the German Tyrker from the wild grapes which were found there, delighted its discoverers by the fruitfulness of the soil, and the mildness of its climate, when compared with Iceland and Greenland. This tract, which was named by Leif the 'Good Vinland' (Vinland it goda), comprised the coast-line between Boston and New York, and consequently parts of the present States of Massachusetts, Rhode Island, and Connecticut, between the parallels of latitude of Civita Vecchia and Terracina, which, however, correspond there only to mean annual temperatures of 47° 8′ and 52° 1′. This was the principal settlement of the Northmen. The colonists had often to contend with a very warlike race of Esquimaux, who then extended further to the south under the name of the Skralinger. The first Bishop of Greenland, Eric Upsi, an Icelander, undertook, in 1121, a Christian mission to Vinland; and the name of the colonized country has even been discovered in old national songs of the inhabitants of the Färoe Islands.

"The activity and bold spirit of enterprise manifested by the Greenland and Icelandic adventurers are proved by the circumstance that, after they had established settlements south of 41° 30′ north latitude, they erected three boundary pillars on the eastern shores of Baffin's Bay, at the latitude of 72° 55′, on one of the Woman's Islands, north-west of the present most northern Danish colony of Upernavik. The Runic inscriptions, which were discovered in the autumn of the year 1824, contain, according to Rask and Finn Magnusen, the date 1135. From this eastern coast of Baffin's Bay, more than six hundred years before the bold expeditions of Parry and Ross, the colonists very regularly visited Lancaster Sound and a part of Barrow's Straits for the purpose of fishing. The locality of the fishing-ground is very definitely described, and Greenland priests from the bishopric of Gardar conducted the first voyage of discovery (1266). This north-western summer station was called Kroksfjardar Heath. Mention is even made of the drift wood (undoubtedly from Siberia) collected there, and of the abundance of whales, seals, walruses, and sea-bears."

Baron von Humboldt has asserted that the merit of first recognizing the discovery of America by the Northmen *belongs indisputably* to Ortelius. The work in which this credit is given the Northmen, the "Theatrum Orbis Terrarum," is a superb illuminated volume, of which the translation was printed in London in 1606; the author's preface is dated Antwerp, 1570. Philip II. of Spain, as we are informed by the biographer, graced Ortelius with the honour and title of the king's cosmographer. A few words from this biography will convey the scope of the author's ambition and ability: "There (at Antwerp) he began to apply himself to benefit succedent ages, to write of those countries by him viewed and seen, to set out in charts and maps divers places both of sea and land unknown to former ages, to describe the tracts and coasts of the east and west, south and north, never spoken of nor touched by Ptolemy, Pliny, Strabo, Mela, or any other historiographer whatsoever." The paragraph in question is this: "But to me it seems more probable, out of the history of the two Zeni, gentlemen of Venice (which I have put down before the table of the South Sea, and before that of Scandia) that this new world many ages past was entered upon by some islanders of Europe, as namely of Greenland, Iceland, and Friesland; being much nearer thereunto than the Indians, nor disjoined thence (as appears out of the map) by an ocean so huge and to the Indians so unnavigable."

An early printed allusion, some say the earliest, to the Norse discovery of America, occurs in Adam of Bremen's " Historia Ecclesiastica Hamburgensis et Bremensis," published at Copenhagen, 1579. The passage referred to is the following, and Mr. Slafter asserts that it was written long before the sagas were reduced to writing: "The same king" (Swein Estrithson, of Denmark, a nephew of Canute the Great) " has besides told us of the discovery of still another island in the midst of the ocean, which is called Vinland, because the grapes grow there spontaneously and give the most glorious wine, also grain, without being sowed, grows there in abundance. This is no fabulous representation, but is founded on the reliable communications of the Danes."

Another early account, and a correct one, of the discoveries of the Scandinavians in the west, was given by Thormod Torfaeus, in his " Historia Vinlandiæ Antiquæ." R. H. Major, who has edited one edition of the letters of Columbus, gives a list of several other ancient authors, Vitalis, Mylius, Grotius, &c., who mention the Scandinavian voyages, and after giving quite a detailed account of them himself, says in conclusion that "no room is left for disputing the main fact of the discovery."

In the Swedish work "Nordbon under Hednatiden" (Norsemen during the Pagan Period), by A. E. Holmberg, there is a curious bit of information: "As late as the year 1347 history can mention a voyage undertaken from Greenland to Vinland. ... This statement is to be found in the Skalholt annals, concluded in the year 1356. Finally we will, as a further proof of our forefathers' knowledge of America long before Columbus' time, mention a world's-chart that was prepared in 1300, where this land is to be found designated under the name Synribygd (southern district). It is to be found in the manuscript of the so-called Rymbegla, and is undoubtedly the oldest map of the globe on which the new world is indicated."

One of the older Swedish historians, Strinnholm, contributes a valuable paragraph: "The whole power of the Northern Vikings was at that time chiefly directed to England, Ireland, Scotland, and other known lands. This, besides the length of the distance, diverted attention from the new discoveries, until finally with the ceasing of the Viking expeditions, all knowledge of the strange unknown land died out, so that only *saga* has preserved the recollection of it. But a vague report of the Norsemen's voyages of discovery penetrated to the Norsemen in France, and through them and their connection with Italy probably also came to the great Italian seaports, and accidentally conduced to awaken and sustain a supposition of unknown lands lying far in the west. So much is certain, however, that the northerly portion of the new part of the world that some centuries afterwards was found by Columbus, had already, toward the close of the tenth century, been discovered by the Scandinavian Vikings, and, as it appears, occupied by a lot of Scandinavian settlers as late as the twelfth century."

The words of the celebrated Swedish historian, E. G. Geijer, must not be omitted in this connection; they are from the great work "Svea rikes häfder" (The Annals of the Kingdom of Sweden): "Viking expeditions, and, as these soon ceased, still more commerce, desire of knowledge, war and court service led them far around, and became to them the means of at once acquiring wealth and glory; although neither royal favour, gifts, or any of the incentives and comforts other countries offered, could hinder them from finally returning to the rocky dales of their native land. But about one hundred years after the arrival of the first settlers on the island, others went over from there to Greenland, and established settlements both on its east and west coasts. They afterwards found, south of Greenland, other coasts, at first full of bare cliffs, farther down more flat and low, finally a good land on a sound, with an island in the north. There the streams were rich in salmon, a kind of grain grew wild, and fruit that resembled grapes, wherefore the first discoverer called the land *Vinland det Goda*. Those who after him sought it, also encountered natives, who bartered furs from them. No permanent connection arose for the rest with this land, which, however, was visited by a Greenland bishop in the year 1121; but without doubt it is some part of the coast of North America which appears in these old Icelandic narratives, five hundred years before Columbus."

All Scandinavian authors on this subject have naturally availed themselves of "the rolls and masses of parchments in the great public and private libraries of Copenhagen and Stockholm." Sometime the modern Scandinavians and the English-speaking race, on both sides of the Atlantic, will realize what a detriment this lingual barrier, which has separated nations essentially one and who once possessed a common tongue, has been to them.

Thomas Carlyle does not say much about the discovery, but it is to the point: "Towards the end of this Hakon's (Hakon Jarl) reign it was that the discovery of America took place (985). Actual discovery, it appears, by Eric the Red, an Icelander; concerning which there has been abundant investigation and discussion in our time."

The next reigning king in Norway, it will be seen, took a particular interest in the new colony in Greenland. "Some years afterwards (after colonizing Greenland) Leif, the son of Eric the Red, went to Norway, where he was favourably received by the reigning king, Olaf Tryggveson, to whom he described the country in such favourable terms that Olaf determined to sustain the new colony. Having been himself recently converted to Christianity, the king was filled with great zeal for the propagation of the faith. He persuaded Leif to be baptized, and sent him back to Greenland accompanied with a missionary, by whose efforts his father Eric and the other colonists were converted." This occurs in Wheaton's "History

F

of the Northmen," and suffices to show how soon both royal and ecclesiastical recognition of the existence of a colony in Greenland followed upon the establishing of the colony. The same is true of Vinland. As many of the Greeks and Romans, Pythias of Marseilles, Pliny the Elder, Tacitus, Procopius, knew of Scandinavia, all Scandinavian events were likely to be carried by lively rumour to the south of Europe, and as Tacitus, the great Roman historian, had already represented the Sviones (Swedes) as "a rich and powerful maritime nation," the people of Southern Europe were prepared to hear of any great naval achievement on their part, whether of conquest or discovery, and must have been constantly on the *qui-vive*.

Snorre Sturleson was another early writer who, soon after Adam of Bremen, corroborated the testimony of the Sagas relative to the Icelandic voyages to America. As the former was a very prominent man and the latter a canon of Bremen, both of these works must have been known in Rome.

As a matter of course, the Howitts confirm the discovery in their "History and Romance of Northern Europe:" "But Europe did not set bounds to their voyages and enterprises. In 861 they discovered Iceland, and soon after peopled it. Thence they stretched still farther west, and discovered Greenland, to which they originally gave the name of Gunbjörnskär, from Gunbjörn, the discoverer. Spite of its wretched climate they colonized it, and proceeding still southward, they struck upon the coast of North America, as it would appear, about the State of Massachusetts. This was towards the end of the tenth century, that is, five hundred years before Columbus reached that country."

Grenville Pigott's testimony corresponds with the rest: "The Norwegians and their descendants discovered and made settlements in Iceland, Greenland, the Orkneys, and, as has been maintained with great semblance of truth, even in America itself."

The American author, Aaron Goodrich, seems to be impatient of any further discussion on the point, regarding it as altogether superfluous, for he says: "The general reader has been convinced of the fact, which is now no longer disputed, that the Northmen were the first modern discoverers of this continent;" while Toulmin Smith is indignant that the claim of Columbus should ever have been considered at all, declaring: "*He was not the discoverer of America in any sense of the term; he did not explore the American continent.*" Referring to Torfœus, this author says that he, Torfœus, derived his information from the original authentic sources, and that "the parchment manuscripts that contain them are, at this moment, in a state of high preservation." This fact is again made known by Prof. Rasmus B. Anderson, in his "America not discovered by Columbus," whose very title is an indignant denial of the claim of the Italian adventurer; he, too, says: "The manuscripts in which we have the Sagas relating to America are found in the celebrated 'Codex Flatoiensis,' a skin-book that was finished in the year 1387. This work, written with great care, and executed in the highest style of art, is now preserved in its integrity in the archives of Copenhagen, and a carefully printed copy of it is to be found in Mimer's Library at the University of Wisconsin." This information is of the greatest importance, for it may be necessary further on, should the advocates of Columbus's claim attempt to force an acknowledgment of it from the people of the United States, for this book to be produced, as irrefragable testimony to the fact of the Norse discovery of America. All translations, reprints, abstracts, may be doubted by the hypercritical, by the class, far too large, who are credulous where they should not believe, and sceptical where they should—there is always more faith than reason in the Christian world—*but the original document cannot be doubted.*

Washington Irving, it appears, did not investigate the subject; if he had done this before commencing his "Life of

Columbus," this work would probably not have been written; to have investigated it afterwards would have exposed him to very uncomfortable feelings, and he was far from foreseeing that the admission of the Columbian discovery would be fraught with unmixed evil for the American people. He is candid enough, however, to confess that he did not look into the matter: "There is no great improbability, however, that such enterprising and roving voyagers as the Scandinavians may have wandered to the northern shores of America, &c., and if the Icelandic manuscripts, said to be of the thirteenth century, can be relied upon as genuine, free from modern interpolation and correctly quoted, they would appear to prove the fact."

It is thought that the lands discovered by Bjarni Herjulfson, the actual first discoverer, gathered from the details and minute description of the voyages, were Connecticut, Long Island, Rhode Island, Massachusetts, Nova Scotia, and Newfoundland. "It may, perhaps, be urged in disparagement of these discoveries," writes Beamish, " that they were *accidental*, that Bjarni Herjulfson set out in search of Greenland and fell in with the eastern coast of North America, but so it was also with Columbus. The sanguine and skilful Genoese navigator set sail in quest of Asia and discovered the West Indies; even when in his last voyage he did reach the eastern shore of Central America, he still believed it to be Asia, and continued under that impression till the day of his death." Washington Irving dwells much upon this curious misconception of Columbus, and the bewilderment and confusion evinced in the " skilful navigator's " own letters is amusing in the extreme.

Another American author, Arthur Gilman, gives expression to a common objection urged by unthinking people against the Norse discovery, namely, that it led to nothing, produced no results. Unfortunately, he is not trying to combat this view; he only presents it as his own: " We have nothing to do here with the expeditions of the Northmen, who are said to have visited America in the eleventh century, for admitting that the records found in the Sagas are true statements of historic facts, their visits did not lead to settlements of lasting importance. To Columbus belongs the undivided honour of first making real the grand idea of the Western World. His discovery led to all that has since been achieved on our continent. ... The legends of the Northmen, whom the Sagas tell us came to these shores five hundred years before Columbus, belong rather to the domain of the antiquary or the poet than to that of the historian."

To render this assertion true, that "their visits did not lead to settlements of lasting importance," it is necessary to blot out of the past the written statements of Adam of Bremen, of Snorre Sturleson, and of Ion Thordarson, who wrote the Sagas of Eric the Red and of Thorfinn Karlsefne, in the "Codex Flatoiensis;" the fact that the rumours of these vast discoveries in the West reached every seaport in southern Europe, as well as the Eternal City; the fact that Gudrid, the wife of Karlsefne, visited Rome after her three years' sojourn in Vinland; the fact that she narrated these experiences at length to the holy fathers; the fact that Rome had appointed bishops to both Greenland and Vinland; the fact that Columbus, an *Italian* by birth, and naturally aware of all these important events, went to Iceland, in order to pursue the investigations to which all this had given him the clue. After his visit to Iceland he made out to find America, as any one else could have found it, after obtaining definite directions. That there was an interval of five hundred years between the first colonization and the subsequent one does not alter the fact that the first one led to the last, was the direct cause of it, and that this was brought about by a close and unbroken sequence of events, every link of which is preserved, that posterity may demonstrate just what grand results have ensued from the discovery and intelligent explorations of the Norsemen, and the full accounts that they recorded of these achievements in Iceland.

CHAPTER IV.

ROMAN CATHOLIC COGNIZANCE OF THE FACT AT THE TIME OF THE NORSE DISCOVERY.

It will not be difficult to prove that the wise-heads in the Eternal City were aware, almost as soon as the Icelanders themselves, that some of the adventurous sons of that race had pushed their explorations clear to remote lands across the ocean, and founded colonies there; it would be far more difficult to prove that they did not know it. Fear, envy, hatred, a deep-seated animosity, made them observant of every move of the Norsemen; these were the only obstacle to the sacerdotal plan of universal sovereignty, of the subjection of all mankind to the rule of the Cross, all Europe was Christianized with the exception of the pagan North; the circle was gradually narrowing around these, and escape from the Papal decree and dominion was impossible. Any discovery made by the Norsemen of new lands, in whatever quarter of the globe, meant the establishing of a new stronghold of paganism, if this discovery should be made unbeknown to Rome. It does not require any knowledge of jesuitical operations, or of the history of the Inquisition, or of heretic-hunts in general, to show one how skilful the Roman Catholic mind is in ferreting out things, what a meddlesome, prying, inquisitive, impertinent, well-trained spy it is, and how quick it is to scent out possible mischief for the Church.

Olaf Tryggveson had already been drawn into the fold of

this Church, thanks to English zeal, when Eric the Red discovered Greenland; consequently when Leif went to Norway with full reports of the new colony and its flourishing condition, King Olaf promptly made up his mind, doubtless with the entire concordance of the Pope, to sustain the colony and establish Christianity there. An extract from the original narrative in the "Heimskringla" best describes this: "The same winter, 999—1000, was Leif, the son of Eric the Red, with King Olaf, in good repute, and embraced Christianity. But the summer that Gissur went to Iceland, (King Olaf sent Leif to Greenland, in order to make known Christianity there; he sailed the same summer to Greenland. He found, in the sea, some people on a wreck, and helped them; the same time discovered he Vinland the Good, and came in harvest to Greenland. He had with him a priest, and other clerks, and went to dwell at Brattahlid with Eric, his father. Men called him afterwards Leif the Lucky; but Eric, his father, said that these two things went one against the other, inasmuch as Leif had saved the crew of the ship, but brought evil men to Greenland, namely the priests." In another version, from the history of Olaf Tryggveson, is added: "But still after the counsel and instigation of Leif, was Eric baptized, and all the people in Greenland." The domestic economy of the Church of Rome was not such that there could have been a new discovery, a colony formed, and a wholesale conversion of the settlers without the Pope and his whole establishment knowing of it, still less when the "Northern barbarians" had made the discovery, formed the colony, and been converted to the true faith. This was occasion enough for a public thanksgiving and when this successful proselyting had been due to a powerful monarch, fired with a holy zeal, and who did not stick at trifles nor call anything a crime that was done in the name of religion, this felicitous conjunction of events was not a thing to pass unnoticed.

The reader will remember the little statement by Baron von Humboldt that "the first Bishop of Greenland, Eric Upsi, an Icelander, undertook, in 1121, a Christian mission to Vinland." Samuel Laing gives details of the spiritual supervision over Greenland, a supervision scarcely compatible with complete Papal ignorance of the existence of a colony there: "The discovery of Greenland by the Icelanders about the year 981, and the establishment of considerable colonies on one or on both sides of that vast peninsula which terminates at Cape Farewell,—in which Christianity and Christian establishments, parishes, churches, and even monasteries were flourishing, or at at least existing to such an extent that from 1124 to 1387 there was a regular succession of bishops, of whom seventeen are named, for their superintendence,—are facts which no longer admit of any reasonable doubt. The documentary evidence of the Sagas,—which gave not merely vague accounts of such a discovery and settlement, but statistical details, with the names and the distances from each other of farms or townships, of which there were, according to accounts of the fourteenth century, ninety in what was called Vestribygd or the western settlement, with four churches, and one hundred and ninety in the Eystribygd or eastern settlement, with one cathedral, eleven other churches, two towns, and three or four monasteries,—bears all the internal evidence of truth, in the consistency and simplicity of the statements."

Strinnholm gives a full description of the settlements in Greenland, of which the abstract is that an Iceland man, Eric Röde, the father of the Leif Ericsson who discovered America, discovered Greenland, and returned in 985 with five-and-twenty ships. After that the emigration to this land increased every year. Within a short time large tracts of the country, both in the east and west, were peopled and settled by Icelandic or Scandinavian settlers. The land's nature and situation divided them into two main colonies, which were called *Oster* and *Vester byggden*. Between them lay a desert, several days' journey long. The chief colony was in Österbyggden, which always remained the most populous and flourishing. In Vesterbyggden there were ninety villages or hamlets, with four or five churches, and in Österbyggden the number of settlements went up to one hundred and ninety, and the churches to twelve, and there were also several cloisters for nuns and monks. The Greenland colony flourished for four hundred years.

Laing gives another important item: "A brief of Pope Nicholas V. in 1448, to the Bishops of Skalholt and Holum in Iceland, states that his beloved children dwelling in an island called Greenland, on the utmost verge of the ocean north of Norway, and who are under the Archbishop of Drontheim, have raised his compassion by their complaint that after having been Christians for six hundred years, and converted by the holy Saint Olaf, and having erected many sacred buildings and a splendid cathedral on said island, in which divine service was diligently performed, they had thirty years ago been attacked by the heathens of the neighbouring coast, who came with a fleet against them, and killed and dispersed many, and made slaves of those who were able-bodied; but having now gathered together again, they crave the services of priests and a bishop."

There was, in short, a regular succession of bishops in Greenland for two hundred and fifty years. We have already seen that mention is made of a voyage from Greenland to Vinland as late as the year 1347. The next link in this most remarkable chain of events is the voyage of Gudrid, Karlsefne's wife, from Vinland to Rome, *viâ* Iceland. Her visit to the holy fathers is described by the French author, Gabriel Gravier, in his work "Découverte de l'Amérique par les Normands:" "Quand elle eut marié Snorre, Gudrida fit un pélerinage à Rome. Elle fut bien reçue et raconta certainement ses voyages dans les contrées ultra océaniques. Rome était très attentive aux découvertes géographiques, collectionnait avec soin les cartes et les récits qui lui parvenaient. Toute découverte semblait un agrandissement du domaine papal, un champ nouveau pour la prédication évangélique. De ce qu'ils n'ont laissé dans l'histoire écrite aucune trace appréciable, les récits de Gudrida n'en exercèrent pas moins sans doute une certaine influence sur les découvertes postérieures."

Thus the part that a woman plays in bringing about the plagiaristic discovery of America is a very important one, and Gudrid, Karlsefne's high-born and intelligent wife, was only excusable in that she did not realize what she was doing, nor the momentous consequences of her act, when she carried such valuable tidings to Rome! The Sagas relate that she went there, so there can be no doubt on that point. In the "Voyages," as translated by Beamish, it is stated thus: "But when Snorre was married, then went Gudrid abroad, and travelled southwards, and came back again to the house of Snorre, her son, and then had he caused a church to be built at Glaumbæ;" and in the synopsis of the historical evidence, by Professor Rafn, it is stated still more explicitly: "His son, Snorre, who had been born in America, was his successor on this estate. When the latter married, his mother made a pilgrimage to Rome, and afterwards returned to her son's house at Glaumbæ, where he had in the meantime ordered a church to be built. The mother lived long as a religious recluse." Gudrid is spoken of in the narratives as "a grave and dignified woman, and therewith sensible, and knew well how to carry herself among strangers." As the widow of a highly-distinguished man, for Thorfinn Karlsefne was "a wealthy and powerful Icelandic merchant, descended from an illustrious line of Danish, Swedish, Norwegian, Irish, and Scottish ancestors, some of whom were kings, or of royal blood," Gudrid was one to carry much influence and must have been listened to in Rome with the most profound attention. Her wealth also conduced to increase the respect with which she was treated by a set of people who have always shown the nicest discrimination in this regard, and when she afterwards became a nun, the Church reaped a double advantage from her sojourn in Vinland. Gudrid had encouraged her husband to colonize Vinland, having always felt the deepest interest in the new country, of which so much was said in Greenland, and with the full prerogative of a Northern woman, a woman there being regarded as her husband's equal, took an active part in the management of affairs and was consulted on every point, consequently she was well versed in all pertaining to Vinland and able to give very accurate information, embracing all possible topographical and geographical details. Exploring expeditions were of frequent occurrence during the three years the colonists stayed in Vinland. By a singular coincidence Karlsefne himself, as stated in the "Voyages," narrated originally the events that occurred on these voyages, this in Iceland, and his wife narrated her experiences—*in Rome;* his narrative, when committed to writing, destined, eight hundred years afterwards, to save the land he attempted to colonize from the disastrous effects of his wife's indiscretion in leading the covetous gaze of the Church to a land so rich in promise and which might become its future empire.

The famous geographer, Malte-Brun, states, in his "Histoire de la Géographie," that Columbus, when in Italy, had heard of the Norse discoveries beyond Iceland, for Rome was then the world's centre, and all information of importance was sent there. It was this some ages before, nay, it was more than this, it was a great whispering-gallery, in which not a word or sound, uttered in any part of the world, that was important for the Church to know, was lost.

Besides the religious means of communication there was the commercial; the Scandinavians carried on an enormous commerce and their peaceful trading-vessels as well as war-dragons ranged the seas. All authors note this with wonder and admiration. To cite Pigott: "It would not be difficult to show that the Scandinavians, from the eighth to the eleventh century, carried on a more active commerce, and could boast a more constant and extensive communication with distant countries, than any other nation of Europe. During the greater part of this period, Russia, Sweden, and Denmark were the only European nations which had any regular commerce with the East." Despising secrecy, and having no motive for it, whatever they did was known to the world; loving fame and glory, seeking these as the highest earthly good, they increased their own celebrity by every means in their power, and each man in his endeavour was aided by the rest of his compatriots, the national pride among them being so great as to destroy all envy, the besetting sin of Christian communities from that day to this. The greatness of each individual conduced to the greatness of his country, and no attempt was made to suppress it.

The Church of Rome knew, knew all that they had accomplished, and every detail concerning the discovery and colonization of Iceland, Greenland, and Vinland! What use did it make of this knowledge?

CHAPTER V.

ALL THE MOTIVES FOR THE CONCEALMENT AND FRAUD.

YES, what use did the Church of Rome make of this knowledge of the discovery of Greenland and Vinland? In the first place it concealed it. As far as is known no writer of southern or middle Europe seems to have made an historical record of the great discovery by the Norsemen except Adam of Bremen, until Snorre Sturleson's "Chronicle of the Kings of Norway" was written, in the thirteenth century, and the two important Sagas relating exclusively to this discovery, contained in the "Codex Flatoiensis," in the fourteenth. Ortelius accorded to them the merit of this discovery in 1570, Mylius in 1611, Grotius in 1642, Diveone in 1643, Montanus in 1671, Torfœus in 1705. We know that Adam of Bremen received his information from King Swein of Denmark, and had very strong Northern sympathies, writing very favourably of the institutions and characteristics of the people, especially of the inhabitants of Sweden; Torfœus based his assertions entirely on the authentic sources in Iceland, and it is presumable that the other early authors mentioned did the same. It is obvious that they wrote with a certain boldness and proclaimed a theory with regard to the discovery of the New World that was new as yet to their contemporaries. It was thus essentially the historians of the North who recorded and proclaimed the great achievement, concerning which the monkish chroniclers were ominously silent.

And who wrote on Scandinavian mythology or gave to the

world any information concerning the religion of Odin, the manners and customs of the people who had a heroic age while the rest of Europe was steeped in slavery and cowardly subjection, and an antiquity as worthy of being called classic as that of Greece itself?[1] Suhm, Nyerup, Schöning, Grundtvig, Thorlacius, Rafn, Finn Magnusen, P. E. Müller, Grater, Abrahamsen, and others. Thorlacius and Finn Magnusen are descendants of Thorfinn Karlsefne, as are also Snorre Sturleson and the famous sculptor, Thorwaldsen; Rafn is a Dane, and there are evidently no Spaniards or Italians in this list. Southern writers, it is plain, held the Northern mythology in as little esteem as the Grecian; both were pagan, and paganism was to be obliterated from both literature and life. We are told by all writers on this subject, with one voice, that "the zealous promoters of Christianity omitted nothing to destroy all relics of the ancient superstition." The resemblance of the Northern mythology to the Grecian was sufficient in itself to kindle Roman Catholic aversion to it, and when it produced a similar type of man, the rage and malice of the morally-deformed race knew no bounds. Could not Rolf, the Norman invader, have stood as the model of an old Greek hero? It is said that "he was mild and gentle toward the poor and oppressed; stern and terrible toward his enemies; but toward his friends faithful and so generous, that he for them spared

---

[1] According to Pigott: "Until the latter end of the sixteenth century, all knowledge of the religion of heathen Scandinavia, possessed by other nations, was confined to what could be gleaned from the works of Paulus Diaconus, Adam of Bremen, and Saxo Grammaticus. The first was a Lombard of the latter end of the eighth century; the second a Canon of Bremen, who wrote in the eleventh; and the last the secretary of Bishop Absalom in the twelfth, more celebrated for the elegance of his Latin and for his classical attainments than for historical correctness, and whose information respecting the Northern mythology is obscured and disfigured by his practice of decorating its deities with the inappropriate names of the gods of Rome."

neither gold nor other valuables; wherefore there were assembled with him the most illustrious warriors of the whole North, and all the neighbouring kings were subordinate to him." And Orvar Odd also, of whom it is related that "he believed neither in Odin, Thor, or any other divinity, but only in his own strength and good-fortune, which is said to have been so great, that if he only hoisted sail, he had favourable winds wherever he went." The learned Swede, Olaf Rudbeck, in his famous work, the "Atlantica," published in 1702, could, without charge of being fantastical or absurd, demonstrate gravely that Sweden was Plato's lost Atlantis. According to the modern Swedish author, August Strindberg, "in the year 1830 Geijer, in the perusal of Homer, comes upon the same idea, or the striking resemblance between 'the customs of the heroic age with the Greeks and Scandinavians.' In his treatise of the same name he shows that which is common in the people's thought and way of life, in laws, institutions, and habits, so that the reader is astonished that he has not before come to the thought himself; but Geijer draws no conclusions from it." We know, too, from history that the Norsemen were great favourites in Greece, the only country in Europe that welcomed them, with the exception of Russia, whose people invited the Swedes to come and rule over them, and that they were the chosen body-guard of the Greek emperors.

In every respect the ancient Scandinavians were the moral antitheses of the Romans or Roman Catholics; and it is no stretch of reason to say that they were the moral antidote of the Southern poison, a fierce remedy used by Nature against the spread of the evil, and yet, as events proved, ineffectual after all against a malaria that had to run its time and can only be killed in our own day by the aid of the very element, the Norse one, first employed against it. The Scandinavians were brave; fear was as unknown to them as courage to the Roman Catholics: accordingly we find on the one hand absolute fearlessness and independence, on the other absolute servility. Mallet delineates this striking trait of the Norse character most admirably: "Thus strongly moulded by the hand of nature, and rendered hardy by education, the opinion they entertained of their own courage and strength must have given the peculiar turn to their character. A man who thinks he has nothing to fear, cannot endure any sort of constraint; much less will he submit to any arbitrary authority, which he sees only supported by human power, or such as he can brave with impunity. As he thinks himself not obliged to court any one's favour or deprecate his resentment, he scorns dissimulation, artifice, or falsehood. He regards these faults, the effects of fear, as the most degrading of all others. He is always ready to repel force by force; hence he is neither suspicious nor distrustful. A declared enemy to his enemy, he attacks openly; he confides in, and is true to others; generous, and sometimes in the highest degree magnanimous, because he places his dearest interest in the idea he entertains and would excite of his courage."

Fear brings so many other vices in its train, that when it is declared that the Norsemen were utterly devoid of fear, one can infer that they were not superstitious or idolatrous, not false, not tolerant of evil, not sophistical in their way of reasoning nor given to the suppression of their convictions, the reverse of which is shockingly true of the Roman Catholics. Not to dwell now on the numerous points of difference, each of which fired their hostility toward each other, it is only necessary to mention in this connection the Norsemen's belief in love between the sexes and deep reverence for it, a belief that the Christian religion immediately expunged from its ethics. Max Nordau defines this in particularly keen language: "The Christian *morale* does not acknowledge that love is legitimate; therefore there is not either, in the institutions that are penetrated by the former, any place left for love. Marriage is now such an institution, its character has betrayed the influence of the Christian *morale*. According to the theological comprehension, marriage has also nothing to do with man's love for woman. If people marry, it is to perform a sacrament, not to belong to each other in love. It would certainly be more agreeable to God if one did not marry at all." Among the Northern race, on the other hand, romance, constancy, devoted love, and chivalrous attachment to the sex so highly honoured, were the atmosphere of their lives. The power of the men was doubled by the fact that the women were always with them in love, sharing their ambition, stimulating them to fresh deeds of glory ; while in the South, women were either shut up in the convents, debauched, or turned into zeros by the thraldom of the mediæval marriage, in which women were only to bear children and bless God. "In paganism," to cite a noble paragraph from Strindberg's "Swedish People," "woman seems almost to have been man's equal. . . . Woman was treated by man with such respect and acted with such self-feeling and freedom, that any such thing in our enlightened times would be considered unheard of." To indicate another respect in which the method of operation in the life of the Norsemen was the opposite of that of his natural foe, these worked to bring about material prosperity, not for a favoured class, but for all the other race worked for pauperism. "In union with commerce," writes A. E. Holmberg, "these celebrated sea-voyages brought here a perfectly incredible wealth, of which it was not possible for us to be deprived during the Christian middle ages, through the plundering system directed against us in all respects."[2] The great Swedish king, Gustaf Vasa, had a threefold task : to free his land from the Danish yoke, to free it

---

[1] "It may be fairly concluded," writes Pigott, "that a people possessing so many sources of wealth, and with such continual communication with the most civilized portions of the world, could not have been so darkly barbarous as the well-grounded detestation of the monkish chroniclers has represented them."

from the jurisdiction of the Pope and from the deep poverty into which five centuries of priest-rule and mediævalism had sunk it. The well-known traveller, Horace Marryat, in his "One Year in Sweden," affirms that poverty was unknown in Sweden until the introduction of Christianity there.[3]

But with all the difference in disposition, character, moral status, the pagan Norsemen and the Roman Catholics had the same visible aim—the conquest of the world. This made them rivals. One desired to obtain dominion to the end of freedom, the other to the end of slavery. Where the former succeeded, they established free institutions, good laws, physical and mental well-being, changing by a rapid metamorphosis, once the monkish hordes were subdued, into benign and able statesmen; where the latter succeeded, they founded cathedrals and monasteries, destroying all law but that of the Church. The scope of their ambition was equal, the motives of it utterly dissimilar.

No wonder then that Hastings was one of the most detested of the Northern leaders! Hated in France, perhaps, as is alleged, "on account of the extent and cruelty of his ravages," but hated still more because of the extent of his ambition, which had made the conquest of Rome its cherished aim. In Wheaton's words: "Hastings proposed to the sons of Ragnar Lodbrok and his other followers an expedition against Rome, of whose wealth and splendour they had heard much, without knowing precisely in what part of Italy the capital of the Christian world was situate." Holmberg's "Norsemen during the Pagan Period"

---

[3] As an illustration of the extent to which Christianity has developed poverty I quote the following paragraph from Felix Oswald's "Secret of the East:" "We do not think it necessary to alleviate the distress of the poor till it reaches a degree that threatens to end it. We have countless benevolent institutions for the prevention of outright death, not one benevolent enough to make life worth living. Infanticide is now far more rigorously punished than in old times. We enforce every child's right to live and become a humble, tithe-paying Christian; but as for its claim to live happy, we refer it to the sweet by-and-by."

contains an interesting passage relative to this; after citing one of the ancient poets of France quoted by Cronholm in his "Norsemen in Vester-viking," he says: "The remarkable part of it is that these high thoughts are put in Hastings' mouth by a *hostile* writer, who lets the terrible Hastings, the most dreaded leader of the Norse expeditions of the ninth century, chant o glory as the highest aim for which he had striven, and that for this hundreds of thousands had fallen under his sword. But there still remained a higher aim, for the winning of which he encouraged his warriors—namely, to let all the kingdoms of the world, which lay open to them, behold their glory, and when they placed the crown of Rome on Björn Jernsida's head, their praise with his should resound around the whole circumference of the earth." When this man was converted it was indeed an occasion for rejoicing among all Romanists; as Wheaton says, "this was an object of the highest interest to the people, who had been so long terrified and distressed by his incursions." This same author, who has a clear perception of the nature of the animosity between the two opposing forces of Europe in those ages, analyzes it still further by saying that after the cruelties practised by Charlemagne, "the great struggle between the North and the South assumed the character of a religious as well as national war, and the enmity of the Scandinavian invaders to the nations they had plundered and vanquished could only be appeased by their own conversion to Christianity, which finally put a period to their predatory incursions." The truth of this also appears in some words of William and Mary Howitt's: "War and plunder, therefore, in their eyes, so far from being in any degree criminal, were acts of glory and of merit. When we read of the bloody Danes, who were, in fact, just as often Swedes or Norwegians, we should remember this, and moreover that they cherished a particular hatred to Rome and to the Christian religion, because it came to them from Rome with all its monks and, what appeared to them, effeminate doctrines."

The fact cannot be too strongly emphasized that the Christianizing of this formidable race was a protective measure for the safety of the Romanists, *not in any sense* a kind or philanthropic work for the good of the Norsemen, for either their temporal or spiritual welfare. The authors just quoted say with great force: "It is not, perhaps, so much an overwhelming number of these Northmen, as the new spirit they brought with them, that mixed with and changed the social elements of the countries they settled in." This spirit could only be destroyed by transforming it into the Christian spirit. The only country in which there has been no admixture, to speak of, of the Norse spirit, is Spain, and Buckle, as we well know, describes the state of things there with absolute correctness in this passage: "These, then, were the two great elements of which the Spanish character was compounded—loyalty and superstition; reverence for their kings and reverence for their clergy were the leading principles which influenced the Spanish mind, and governed the march of Spanish history." It is obvious that the Church of Rome had a superhuman work before it to reduce Scandinavia to such a condition as that. The time it took to bring about consent to baptism, a concession which did not mean as much as it seemed, was incalculable; Laing mentions the startling fact that "this last remnant of paganism among the European people existed in vigour almost five hundred years after Christianity and the Romish Church establishment were diffused in every other country." One reason of this was, as averred by Geijer, that the Christian ethics were so unlike the pagan, and put bonds upon the individual freedom to which the Northerner was not willing to subject himself; another was that the Scandinavians had no respect for the people who professed Christianity, no admiration for their institutions; another, that there was so very little superstition in their nature for the priests to work upon. The following anecdotes illustrate this: "When St. Olaf proposed to Gauka Thor to be baptized, the chief answered that he and his comrades were neither Christians nor heathens, but trusted to their own courage, strength, and fortune, with which until then they had had every reason to be satisfied; but if the king was very anxious they should believe on some god, they were as well content to believe in the white Christ as on any other. Arnliot Gellina told the same king that he had always been wont to put his trust in nothing but his own strength, which had never failed him, and that he had now thought to trust in the king; but since he (the king) was so desirous that he should be baptized, although he was not aware of what the white Christ was capable of performing, for the king's sake he would believe on him." Pigott, who relates these highly characteristic stories, continues: " It was also said of Hrolf Krake and his warriors, at a much earlier period, that they never offered to the gods, but relied on their own strength. Some, although uninstructed in the doctrines of Christianity, rejected the superstitions of their countrymen from more exalted motives." So he justly argues in this wise: " The difficulties, therefore, which the first preachers of Christianity in Scandinavia had to encounter, may be attributed rather to the contempt in which these lawless warriors held a creed which threatened them with a life of peace and inactivity, than to barbarous ignorance, or even to any bigoted adherence to their ancient religion." In short, the ancient Scandinavians, like the ancient Greeks, left the worship of the gods to the superstitious lower classes. It was reserved for the Christian nations of modern times, and the free United States, to elevate this idolatry into the devout practice of refined and cultivated people.

Laing, who has made a deep study of this subject, states that "the churches or temples of Odin appear to have had no consecrated order of men like a priesthood set apart for administering in religious rites," and that "public worship under any form, or private or household devotion in the Odin religion, cannot be distinctly traced in the Sagas." In commenting on this, he says: "We find in the North very few remains of temples; no statues, emblems, images, symbols; was it actually more spiritual than any other systems of paganism, and, therefore, less material in its outward expression?"

A comparison of the pagan festival Jul with the Christian festival Yule (Christmas) after the Romanists had incorporated it into their system and remodelled it, will illustrate the difference in the mode of worship, as it is called, of these two races. The Norse festival is thus described by Beamish: "Yule was a pagan festival, celebrated in honour of Thor, at the beginning of February, when the Northmen's year commenced, and they offered sacrifices for peace and fruitful seasons to this deity; it lasted fourteen days. . . . After the introduction of Christianity, the anniversary of Yule was transferred to Christmas, which is still called by that name throughout Scandinavia." And by Mallet thus: "There were three great religious festivals in the year. The first was celebrated at the winter solstice. They called the night on which it was observed the Mother Night, as that which produced all the rest; and this epoch was rendered the more remarkable as they dated from thence the beginning of the year, which among the Northern nations was computed from one winter solstice to another, as the month was from one new moon to the next. This feast, which was very considerable, was named Jul, and was celebrated in honour of Frej, or the sun, in order to obtain a propitious year and fruitful seasons."

So little weight did the Northern people attach to baptism, when the proselyters, by dint of arduous efforts, had at last got them that far, that a story is told of one man who was baptized twenty times. As Laing observes: "Christianity in Scandinavia seems, in the eleventh century, to have consisted merely in the ceremony of baptism, without any instruction in its doctrines." It seemed in many instances to have been merely the deference that well-bred people, when travelling in foreign lands, pay to the natives of the country they happen to be in, to judge from this remark of Wheaton's: "On their return to their native country, they made no scruple to conform to the external practices of heathenism, believing that Thor, and the other deities of the North, were to be adored as the local gods of Norway, in the same manner as Christ was worshipped in England as the national god of that country."

However, converted they were, after a long struggle and a sanguinary one. Expressing his satisfaction over this, as befitted a canon, Adam of Bremen says naïvely: "For the rest, the opinion has already become prevalent with the people, that the god of the Christians is the strongest, and that one is often cheated by the other gods, but that this god is always near as a sure and timely help." It is not clear whether by "god" he means Christ or the Supreme Being, but, at any rate, it is plain that the new religion was an experiment, that it was only taken on trial. The following paragraph of Oswald's— "The so-called Christian countries of Northern Europe were not converted before the eleventh century of our era, and revolted in time to prevent their utter ruin"—shows that the experiment was not altogether a satisfactory one, and that *the old troubles had broken out afresh*. To make a condensed statement of the first protest of the Scandinavian North against the supremacy of Rome, Gustaf Vasa, in Sweden, again demonstrated the opposite tendency of the North from that of the South by eradicating Roman Catholicism in Sweden simultaneously with Philip II.'s eradication of Protestantism in Spain. In about ten years the last vestige of the Reformation disappeared in Spain, but in less time than that the spirit of Romanism was banished from Sweden, and Norway and Denmark were scarcely less vigorous in expelling it. Philip II. declared that "it was better not to reign at all than to reign over heretics;" Gustaf I. declared by his acts that he would only reign over free men, and that neither he nor his subjects owed allegiance to Rome.

On the presumption, however, that the conversion of the

pagan North to Christianity was a genuine one, the Romish Church proceeded to obliterate all traces of this abominable paganism which had so long defied it; its notorious acts in Greece were repeated throughout the length and breadth of Scandinavia; submission to it had naturally not abated its hatred, there was still retribution to wreak on the contumacious race that had baffled it, scorned it; all the descendants of this race, for generations to come, should be made to feel the implacable wrath of the outraged power that has its seat in the Eternal City. Having control of literature, a ready means offered itself. The Church could corrupt history, brand the memory of the Norsemen eternally, by representing all their deeds as those of ferocious, bloodthirsty barbarians, by accusing them of such foul crimes as would pale the crimes of the Church, and by systematically concealing all achievements of theirs, of whatever nature, that would awaken the admiration or gratitude of posterity. *The discovery of the New World by the Norsemen was the one event that must most sedulously be concealed!*

We can note Papish operations, step by step, through the centuries; the conversion or amalgamation of the Northern pagans into Christian subjects, of free soil into Church territory, of pagan festivals into religious holidays, of Norse deeds into the means of gratifying the Romanists' inordinate desire for power,—this is the fell work that has been accomplished through the ages. And the consummation of this iniquity was reserved for the nineteenth century, to be out-worked on American soil!

All authors and historians not party to the plot, those of liberal ideas, and who advocate the truth, have openly regretted that history has been made the means of concealing or perverting the truth in regard to the great religious struggle of Europe, and particularly of the Northern race who so valiantly defended the liberty that the sane, natural, healthy man, in possession of his full powers, holds so dear, against the combined assaults of the *anti-naturalists*,—the best name, all things considered, that has been given to the Roman Catholic or Christian body. This definition has been applied by Felix Oswald, who in further elucidation says, "Only anti-natural religions have achieved that deep abasement of the physical type of our race which we see in China and Southern Europe," and expresses an undeniable truth in the assertion : " The night of the Middle Ages was not the natural blindness of unenlightened barbarians, but an unnatural darkness, maintained by an elaborate system of spiritual despotism, and in spite of the fierce struggles of many light-loving nations." But have the Romanists themselves ever deplored this horrible condition of darkness and degradation ? Has not Spain, the spot where the black darkness concentrated, been held up as the model of Christian excellence, for other nations to emulate ? Has any effort ever been made by the Church of Rome to abate this darkness, to infuse health into its morally-diseased votaries ? Has not this, in every instance, been the work of heresy ! The Romanists did not even suspend their efforts when the limit of human misery seemed to have been reached ; there was still an unattained depth beyond, for which they strove with a hellish frenzy ! In Oswald's words : " But the efforts of the spoilers did not cease ; and it may be doubted if the Caucasian race will ever wholly recover from the effects of a thousand years' attempt to lure their children from earth to ghost-land, to poison their minds with the dogmas of pessimism, to sacrifice the pagan Elysium to the Buddhistic Nirvana."

The caution cannot be repeated too often against placing credence in monkish records of the acts of their Scandinavian enemies ; several warnings are given by Beamish : " From the eighth to the eleventh centuries the Northmen carried on a more active commerce, and a more extensive maritime communication with foreign countries than any other nation in Europe. Such intercourse appears quite incompatible with that extreme degree of ignorance and barbarity in which so many writers would clothe all their actions and enterprises ;" and in another place he writes: "We should receive with caution all statements upon a subject to which national or religious feeling is likely to have given an exaggerated colouring. Our knowledge of the excesses of the Northern invaders is chiefly derived from the evidence of monkish chroniclers, whose Christian faith and feelings were no less outraged by the deeds than the infidelity of the pagan ravagers, and who, writing in many cases long after the events, would naturally aid defective evidence with a fervid zeal and fertile imagination." Buckle has been peculiarly observant of this uniform vitiation of historical accounts, and traces the operation of the same causes even up in the North: "But in the ninth and tenth centuries Christian missionaries found their way across the Baltic, and introduced a knowledge of their religion among the inhabitants of Northern Europe. Scarcely was this effected, when the sources of history began to be poisoned." His "History of Civilization" is no more nor less than the history of the conflict of science, invention, research, enlightenment, with the theological system that was against everything but bigotry and idolatry, substituting the debasing worship of the Cross for the true aim of human existence.

The concealment of the Norse discovery of America was the negative part of the Romanists' work; when Christopher Columbus, a nameless Italian adventurer, appeared upon the scene of action, their positive work began, namely, the substitution of another discoverer for the original ones, and a transfer of all the benefits of the Norse discovery to the Roman Catholic power: the foundation had been laid; they would now raise the superstructure. Columbus was a particularly obscure man; no one knew where he was born,—"the question of Columbus' birthplace has been almost as hotly contested as that of Homer," remarks Arthur Helps; no one knew what he had been doing in Italy before he went to Spain, after the idea of making a great discovery had taken full possession of him, and of course the Church kept its own counsels. That august institution has always been blessed with a long memory and was not likely to have forgotten Gudrid's visit, nor the various reports of the Norsemen's voyages that had reached Rome as the world's centre, and been duly recorded, and the recollection of the hated fact, which might after all be turned to account, had been burned into the minds of Popes and prelates for those five centuries by the anxious labour of preventing the remotest allusion to it from getting into any annals.

Columbus made his way to Spain, whether with or without instructions from Rome may be left to conjecture. "Spain at that time," as the Roman Catholic author, Barry, proudly boasts, "commanded the destinies of the whole Catholic world; her struggle against the Koran, the zeal of her crusade undertaken on the soil of Europe, excited the sympathies of the whole Christian world." Columbus went to Spain, from Italy, *after he had made his visit to Iceland*. It is altogether contrary to reason to infer, because this trip to Iceland was kept a profound secret to the world, that the heads of the Church were not privy to it. This knowledge of theirs of his visit to the place where all the information concerning the Norse voyages was preserved, his access to the archives of Iceland, his consultations with Christian prelates there, especially Bishop Magnus, who could put him in the way of learning all he required,—all this was the cause of the absolute secrecy maintained. There is more than sufficient evidence that the wily Italian obtained all that he sought in Iceland; his discovery of America proves that; hence to go to Spain was his next practical move, and entirely in order. He found himself one day, whether by chance or no can be imagined, at the gates of the monastery of La Rabida, in Andalusia, the guardian of which, Juan Perez de Marchina, had formerly been the confessor of Queen Isabella; if this was only a chance, it must be confessed that it was an exceedingly lucky one! Barry describes the meeting; the mere thought of it kindles his Roman Catholic ardour: "He welcomed fraternally the stranger, towards whom he felt a sudden attraction. A kind of intimacy immediately took place between them; for already before their meeting there pre-existed between them the strictest conformity of ideas that can unite two intelligences. The Father Superior, after the first disclosures of Columbus" (*what were those disclosures?*), "invited him to remain with him, the present moment not being favourable to present his project to the Court."

These are very strong words : "*the strictest conformity of ideas that can unite two intelligences ;* " an invitation after *the first disclosures* of Columbus to remain there. Now an exposition of Columbus' scientific theories (so called) as to a probable land in the Western ocean would have required hours, and after the hours spent in this way, the strictest conformity of ideas would not have been induced, for the strictest conformity of ideas was not wont to ensue upon such a talk between a scientist and the Superior of a monastery, assuming Columbus to have been a scientist. After the first disclosures,—had these been merely a rough sketch of a profound scientific theory, there would not have been an invitation which meant so much, that meant, in fact, active co-operation ; but assuming as an hypothesis, that Columbus informed Juan Perez briefly of his visit to Iceland and the satisfactory results from it, of *the absolute certainty* that there was another world lying across the ocean, and of the great good that would accrue to the Church if this land was taken possession of through his (Columbus') instrumentality, the prompt interest and zeal of the priest will be fully accounted for. This is only a surmise, to be sure, but a surmise that has a startling resemblance to truth.

But to continue the narrative : " Between Columbus and his host nobody intervened. The confidence of Father Juan Perez was complete, because the demonstration was peremptory,— because the grand mission of the stranger was manifest to him. . . . He heard, he comprehended, he believed.

". . . The Franciscan recognized in Columbus the mark of a providential election." Doubtless, for Columbus exhibited the craft and secretiveness, the unscrupulous ambition of the religious body to which he belonged; he had proved himself the proper man for the work, the most audacious fraud that was ever perpetrated, and the Church accepted him unconditionally! Columbus was a man who did not let his left hand know what his right hand did, and this was a prime qualification!

He obtained substantial aid in his huge undertaking—it was a huge undertaking to push this scheme through on frail scientific grounds, on account of the necessity of concealing the true grounds from all but a few chosen confidants—from the Grand Cardinal of Spain, Pedro Gonzalez de Medona, through whose intervention, according to Parry's allegation, he procured an audience. Washington Irving, however, states that it was Luis de St. Angel, receiver of the ecclesiastical revenues in Aragon, who overcame the scruples of the queen, and gives his eloquent appeal: "He reminded her of how much might be done for the glory of God, the exaltation of the Church, and the extension of her own power and dominion. What cause of regret to her, of triumph to her enemies, of sorrow to her friends, should this enterprise, thus rejected by her, be accomplished by some other power! He reminded her what fame and dominion other princes had acquired for their discoveries; here was an opportunity to surpass them all. He entreated her Majesty not to be misled by the assertion of learned men, that the project was the dream of a visionary. He vindicated the judgment of Columbus, and the soundness and practicability of his plans." This he could safely do, for he had the strongest material grounds for relying on Columbus' judgment, or rather the trustworthy evidence that Columbus had brought with him from Iceland of the existence of the New World.

Then follows the affecting scene that has elicited so much admiration for Queen Isabella: " With an enthusiasm worthy of herself and the cause, Isabella exclaimed, 'I undertake the enterprise for my own crown of Castile, and will pledge my jewels to raise the necessary funds.'" Irving, who is an extremely romantic writer, exclaims: "This was the proudest moment in the life of Isabella; it stamped her renown for ever as the patroness of the discovery of the New World." But St. Angel said that *he* was ready to advance the necessary funds, for he evidently knew a few things that had not been confided to the queen, and Roman Catholic (perhaps Jesuit) [1] as he was, he realized that knowledge was better than faith, at least in this instance. On this basis of *knowledge* he pledged the funds.

"Armed with these royal commissions," writes Arthur Helps, who also describes the occurrences at the monastery in detail, "Columbus left the Court for Palos; and we may be sure that the knot of friends at the monastery were sufficiently demonstrative in their delight at the scheme on which they had pinned their faith being fairly launched."

Christopher Columbus discovered America, in the year 1492, *in the way described*. Then history, pliant, ductile history, had a new office to perform: to extol Columbus and immortalize him! The monkish chroniclers did this with as little scruple as they had consigned the true discoverers to oblivion.

Aaron Goodrich, who has made a very close study of the character of Columbus, arrives at conclusions in regard to him that will clearly demonstrate to the mind of any candid and unprejudiced reader the reason why Barry, the Roman Catholic, should say of him: "This man had no defect of character, or no worldly quality; we have weighty reasons for considering him a saint." But Goodrich gives a contrary analysis: "By representing himself as the chosen of God, the champion of the Christian religion, carrying the light of the Gospel to heathen nations, by performing the smallest acts with affectation of religious ceremony, by inserting Scriptural and religious sentences in his most trivial letters, by recounting miracles and interviews with God, by giving, in fact, a religious colouring to all his acts, he became the *protégé* of the Church, which has continued through all after centuries to regard him as one of her most zealous votaries, and is now strenuously urged to place him among her saints."

After citing the remark of Lord Klingsborough—"The writing of history, as far as regards the New World, was by the law of Spain restricted to men in priestly orders"—Goodrich performs much-needed service by placing before the public, as a specimen of the exactions, the list of licences that were appended to a small work on Mexico, by Boturini:—

"1. The declaration of his faith.
"2. The licence of an Inquisitor.
"3. The licence of the Judge of the Supreme Council of the Indies.
"4. The licence of the Jesuit father.
"5. The licence of the Royal Council of the Indies.
"6. The approbation of the qualificator of the Inquisition.
"7. The licence of the Royal Council of Castile.

"Beyond all this the person must be of sufficient influence to obtain the favourable notice of the bodies thus represented. Nor was this the end of the difficulty; the licence of any one of these officials could be revoked at pleasure; and, when republished, the work had to be re-examined. The penalty attached to the possession of a book not thus licensed, was death. Such was the tyranny," he adds, "which weighed upon historical writers; and it is not difficult to perceive how all these censors would deal partially with Columbus."

An especial adaptation had to be made to the case; the New World was a dangerous subject altogether, which had to be handled with extreme caution; the difficulty was not only to preserve the fame of Columbus from all heretical cavil, but to rigorously exclude from the pages of history all hint that

Columbus might have had predecessors who were more justly entitled to the fame he reaped.

"To ecclesiastical tyranny and popular prejudice," continues Goodrich, "may be added the exaggerations and falsehoods of the chief actor of the scene;" Columbus' visit to Iceland is the key that reveals all these exaggerations and falsehoods, and many of these were born of the difficulty of keeping his own secret. He quotes Aristotle, Ptolemy, St. Isadore, Bede, Strabo, Petrus Comestor, St. Ambrose, Scotus, Pliny, Nicolas de Lira, St. Augustine, Marinus, and the Holy Scriptures, but not once the "Codex Flatoiensis" the manuscript finished as late as 1395, which contained full information about the new land he sought, and recent information at that. As a specimen of his policy, I quote an extract from one of his letters: "Much more I would have done, if my vessels had been in as good condition as by rights they ought to have been. This is much, and praised be the eternal God, our Lord, who gives to all those who walk in His ways victory over things which seem impossible; of which this is signally one, for although others may have spoken or written concerning these countries, it was all mere conjecture, as no one could say that he had seen them—it amounting only to this, that those who heard listened the more, and regarded the matter rather as a fable than anything else.

Only a few years after this well-attested (?) discovery of the New World, Sweden's period of greatness began; in 1527 King Gustaf I. proclaimed Lutheranism the State religion of Sweden; his son, Carl IX., defeated the attempt of the Catholic reaction, of which Spain was the soul, to re-establish Romanism in Sweden; his grandson, Gustaf Adolf, was one of the leading generals in the "Thirty Years' War," which effected the victory of the Reformation in Europe; in 1776, the American colonies, which had been growing apace in these three centuries, declared independence of Great Britain, and—the severest stroke in the succession of hard strokes that had befallen the Church of Rome—

established a purely secular government! The old Norse spirit, supposed to have been effectually quenched in the year 1000, had broken out again, proven itself indestructible. It had again given Sweden good warriors, good statesmen, good kings and generals; the country doomed to mediæval obscurity and penance, again stepped to the front and made itself felt as a power in Europe, but, worse than all else, it made of the new American Republic the most formidable power for good that the powers of darkness, incarnate in the Church, had ever had to contend with, and this occupied an immense territory, rich, fertile, comprising enormous resources, and admirably calculated to promote enlightenment and the well-being not only of its own inhabitants, but of the down-trodden, oppressed, priest-ridden, pining, inhabitants of Europe! No nation, since the Scandinavian North had devoted itself to glory, had ever been so proud as the American Republic, so boastful of its liberty, its grandeur, its advancement, so impatient of the slightest touch upon its freedom, its rights. No people were so little disposed to bow to either Church or throne, indeed they made a national proclamation of their determination *not* to bow to anything. Norse defiance flamed up again in the person of free-born Americans. The greatest possible progress was threatened in republicanism and free ideas!

What did the Church of Rome do, what *could* it do but claim the United States as its own, on the score of the discovery of America by Columbus? If this claim could be pressed, if the United States could be forced or cajoled into an acknowledgment of the discovery by Columbus, all might be retrieved. But the Church must move with all prudence, the design must not be suspected until fairly accomplished. There was no reason to doubt that the United States would fall into the trap.

Barry remarks a revival of interest and of biographies of Columbus at the beginning of this century, and names Luigi Bossi, Navarrete, W. Irving, and Denis as being instrumental in

H

the favourable reaction. He boasts of his own book, "The Cross in the Two Worlds," as having "come to reveal for the first time the providential mission confided to Columbus, and to affirm loudly the saintliness of his character." An ascending series of publications, he declares, "show the progressive interest that is attached to the memory of Columbus." In lamenting the past injustice to Columbus, for his keen perception seems to have detected something resembling this even in Spain, he avers devoutly that "the Roman Pontificate alone preserved the thought of the apostolic grandeur of Columbus; successively three Popes had honoured with their confidence this herald of the Cross; the Holy See never failed in its regard for him." *We can well believe that!* "But in our days," he cries jubilantly, "there is manifested a movement of reparative justice and friendliness for the fame of Columbus. Pains are taken to honour him."

The plot once clearly discerned, these pains will be taken in vain. It cannot but be apparent to one who gives the subject a moment's serious consideration, that the Church that has fought the Scandinavians for ages in Europe, is not likely to fraternize or coalesce with American institutions that are the natural outgrowth of the Scandinavian spirit. There is a new conflict impending in the United States. The same people who were compelled to abolish the physical slavery of which the seeds were sowed by Spain, will now have to abolish the spiritual slavery which Spain and Rome with combined force are endeavouring to fasten upon it.

In finding fault with the four biographers of Columbus, Spotorno, Irving, Navarrete, and Alex. von Humboldt, who, as he declares, "denaturalize his person and his providential *rôle*," Barry writes this pregnant sentence: "The biography of Columbus has remained in the hands of his natural enemies . . . whence it follows that the view taken of it by Protestantism is the only one by which people have judged of the most vast, and evidently the most superhuman achievement of Catholic genius."

Yes, he is right, the whole plot is most assuredly the most vast and the most superhuman achievement of Catholic genius! What but *Catholic genius*, the genius for deceit, for trickery, for secrecy, for wicked and diabolical machinations, could have pursued such a system of fraud for centuries as the one now being exposed! What but Catholic genius, a prolific genius for evil, would have attempted to rob the Norsemen of their fame, of the knowledge of their great discovery, and to foist a miserable Italian adventurer and upstart upon Americans as the true candidate for these posthumous honours, the man, or saint, to whom they are to do homage, and through this homage allow the Church of Rome to slip the yoke of spiritual subjection over their necks!

One of the most interesting pages in history, the history as yet unwritten, will be the account of the manner in which the American people, the descendants of the Vikings, treat this attempt!

CHAPTER VI.

COLUMBUS' VISIT TO ICELAND.

THE best proof that Columbus went to Iceland, before perfecting his plans for the discovery of the land the other side of the Western ocean, is that he said so himself. The pregnant passage is quoted by Irving, in his "Life of Columbus:" "While the design of attempting the discovery in the West was maturing in the mind of Columbus, he made a voyage to the North of Europe. Of this we have no other memorial than the following passage, extracted by his son from one of his letters: 'In the year 1477, in February, I navigated one hundred leagues beyond Thule, the southern part of which is seventy-three degrees distant from the equator, and not sixty-three, as some pretend; neither is it situated within the line which includes the west of Ptolemy, but is much more westerly. The English, principally those of Bristol, go with their merchandise to this island, which is as large as England. When I was there, the sea was not frozen, and the tides were so great as to rise and fall twenty-six fathom.'"

This statement, according to Professor R. B. Anderson, is also to be found in chapter four of the biography which the son of Christopher Columbus wrote of his father, and which was published in Venice in 1571. Its title is "Vita dell' admiraglia Christoforo Columbo."

Professor Anderson's book, "America not discovered by

HVALFJORDARBOTN, HISTORIC SCENERY NEAR REYKJAVIK.

Columbus," aside from its bold negation of the proud pontifical assertion that the saint in question did discover that country, leads attention to a point that has been almost entirely overlooked, namely, the connection between the *true* and the *alleged* discovery; he says: "While the various writers here alluded to" (he goes over the ground pretty thoroughly) " freely admit the fact that the Norsemen, as well as others, discovered and explored parts of America long before Columbus, they are unwilling to believe that there is any historical connection between the discovery of the Norsemen and that of Columbus; or, in other words, that Columbus profited in any way by the Norsemen's knowledge of America. This is all the more singular since none of them even try to deny the statement made by Fernando Columbo, his son, that he (Christopher Columbus) not only spent some time in Iceland, in 1477, but sailed 300 miles beyond, which must have brought him nearly within sight of Greenland. We are informed that he was an earnest student, and the best geographer and map-maker of his day. He was a diligent reader of Aristotle, Seneca, and Strabo. Why not also of Adam of Bremen, who, in his volume published in the year 1076, gave an accurate and well-authenticated account of Vinland (New England)?" He goes on to say that he believes that "Columbus was a scholar who industriously studied all books and manuscripts that contained any information about voyages and discoveries; that his searching mind sought out the writings of Adam of Bremen, that well-known historian who in the most unmistakable and emphatic language speaks of the Norse discovery of Vinland; that the information thus gathered induced him to make his voyage to Iceland."

Aaron Goodrich, on the other hand, does not believe that Columbus went to Iceland, notwithstanding Columbus wrote about his visit there to his son and his son quoted the passage in his letter,—and he doubts this for the very reason that should have made him credit it implicitly, namely, because

Columbus *has so very little to say about it.* Goodrich comments: "He does not give any reasons for such a voyage (to Iceland) nor mention the ship he sailed in, or the port he sailed from; he gives nothing, in fact, but the most vague assertions. All contemporary writers, State papers, &c., are silent upon the subject, when less important matters are recorded." It is astonishing that so shrewd a writer as Goodrich, who seems to have fathomed Columbus' motives in all other regards, should have expected him to give his reasons for the voyage, mention the ship he sailed in and the port he sailed from, when he was going on a secret expedition, probably commissioned by the Pope himself, for the purpose of stealing knowledge that would put the Church in possession of a vast new territory for the acquisition of gold, slaves, and souls! This secrecy is *prima-facie* evidence that he went to Iceland. But it would have been better for the Church of Rome if his son had burned this letter as soon as he had read it! On so slight a thread, on this little indiscretion of his in keeping the letter and mentioning it, rested the vindication of the fame of the Norsemen and the conviction of Columbus of a base fraud!

Barry, however, does not seem to doubt that Columbus went to Iceland. He writes in his usual ecstatic way: "We see him crossing the German Ocean and advancing to the Polar Seas. In February, 1474, he was a hundred leagues beyond Iceland, and verified some phenomena interesting to hydrography. From the sombre horizons of the North, from the *Ultima Thule* of the ancients to the splendid skies of the tropics"—the writer does not hint at what Columbus verified in Iceland *besides* phenomena—"with his powerful faculty of generalization, he united together in his memory the harmonies of land and sea, seeking to penetrate beyond the poetry of appearances the great laws of the globe." This is not very lucid, but it is suggestive. There is nothing so good to hide a little hard fact as a lot of rhapsodical vapour. Far from seeking to penetrate the great laws of the globe at that precise period, the Italian mariner, who, failing of being a skilful one, was bent on being a lucky one, was on the hunt for those particular paragraphs, in some old manuscript or other, that would serve him as a chart to the coveted land in the West. This is only one evidence more of the elaborate disguise that was thrown around all his movements while at Iceland.

R. H. Major, in the introduction to "Columbus' Letters," mentions the fact of his having gone to Iceland, yet adds: "But upon the whole of this portion of his history there rests an impenetrable cloud of obscurity." It was indeed like a secret of the confessional, divulged only to the holy fathers themselves!

Arthur Helps, in his "Life of Columbus," asserts positively; "We are sure that he traversed a large part of the known world, that he visited England, that he made his way to Iceland and Friesland (where he may possibly have heard vague tales of the discoveries by the Northmen in North America), that he had been at El Mina, on the coast of Guinea, and that he had seen the islands of the Grecian Archipelago." And there can scarcely be anything more emphatic than the following words by Toulmin Smith: "There can be little doubt that he (Columbus) had gained the chief confirmation of his idea of the existence of *terra firma* in the Western ocean, during the visit which he is known to have made, before his Western voyage, to Iceland."

It was on the coast of Guinea, as Goodrich has ascertained, that Columbus qualified himself in a branch of trade that he evidently considered indispensable in the future founder of a colony, for Goodrich states: "For some years, it is unknown at what precise period, Columbus was engaged in the Guinea slave-trade, in which he subsequently showed himself such an adept with regard to the unfortunate Indians as well to deserve the compliment paid him by Mr. Helps, who calls his proceedings and plans worthy of a practised slave-dealer." Professor Anderson states, for the benefit of those who have not read Goodrich's book, "History of the Character and Achievements of the so-called Christopher Columbus," that "Aaron Goodrich pronounces Columbus a fraud, and denounces him as mean, selfish, perfidious and cruel. He has evidently made a very careful study of the life of Columbus, and we have looked in vain for a satisfactory refutation of his statements." Still less can the following statement, by the same author, be refuted: "Columbus owes most of his fame to the Church, which, charmed with the devotion he professed, has chanted his praises, and crushed any historian who would not join in them, as long as her power was sufficient."

The next thing necessary for a full understanding of this momentous visit of Columbus to Iceland is to know the full extent of his opportunities there and the use he made of them. Much light is thrown on this by Laing; in his "Sea-kings of Norway" he makes substantially the same statement as the one quoted in the first chapter of this book; it is this: "It is evident that the main fact is that of a discovery of a Western land being recorded in writing between 1387 and 1395; and whether the minor circumstances, such as the personal adventures of the discoverers, or the exact localities in America which they visited, be or be not known, cannot affect this fact,—nor the very strong side-fact that eighty years after this fact was recorded in writing, in no obscure manuscript, but in one of the most beautiful works of penmanship in Europe, Columbus came to Iceland, from Bristol, in 1477, on purpose to gain nautical information, and must have heard of the written accounts of discoveries recorded in it." The writer also cites the paragraph in the memoir of Columbus by his son. Professor Anderson says, very pertinently, that "there were undoubtedly people still living whose grandfathers had crossed the Atlantic, and it would be altogether unreasonable to suppose that he (Columbus), who was constantly studying and talking about geography and navigation, possibly could visit Iceland and not hear anything of the land in the West." He goes rather farther than other authors, but still does not express himself as severely as the case deserves, when he says: "The fault that we find with Columbus is, that he was not honest and frank enough to tell where and how he had obtained his previous information about the lands which he pretended to discover; that he sometimes talked of himself as chosen of Heaven to make this discovery, and that he made the fruits of his labours subservient to the dominion of Inquisition." This is undeniably a very grave charge, yet it far from characterizes the religious felony of which Columbus was guilty: he purloined the knowledge of a discovery of transcendent value made by men of a pagan race, but recently and very reluctantly converted to Christianity, for the purpose of securing princely honours and emolument for himself, the greatest conceivable aggrandizement for the Church, such an opportunity for universal dominion as could never, in the nature of things, occur again in the life of the world; and last and most important of all, for the purpose of making the New World, through its entire submission to the Holy See, the means of crushing out all tendencies to rebellion against the Church that might possibly manifest themselves again in Europe. The sway of the Church of Rome could not be complete without the acquisition of this new territory, of which the natives were to be forced into allegiance and which was to be colonized only by those firm in the faith. It is utterly impossible for this deed to be understood in all its enormity by those who shrink from regarding it as a religious crime, the most heinous one of the long list that the Church of Rome has committed, and which was to have been the glorious reward for all the others, emblazoning the favourite maxim of this hierarchy, "*The end sanctifies the means,*" on the very skies! Christians of every sect, Protestants of all grades, treat Roman Catholicism very tenderly, for they cannot strike it at any of its vulnerable points, without striking that which is almost equally vulnerable in their own system of religion. Romanism creeps in everywhere under the cover of Protestantism; Protestantism, whatever bears the name of Christianity, is its best shield and defence—in fact its sole one. It is only by regarding Christianity as *one*, of which Romanism is the full expression, and Protestantism the diluted, the component parts of this being, when analyzed, Roman Catholicism and liberality, the first not less evil, intrinsically, through the mixture, the latter only rendered less effective,—and by realizing the atrocious way in which Christianity was introduced in every land, and in every colony—by noting its deadly effects upon every race that were forced to succumb to it, that one can understand the full nature of the crime under consideration. Now, however, the issue can no longer be evaded!

That Columbus had abundant opportunities, in Iceland, to pursue his inquiries is shown clearly by Beamish, in his "Discovery of America by the Northmen:" "Nor should it be forgotten that Columbus visited Iceland in 1477, when, having had access to the archives of the island and ample opportunity of conversing with the learned there through the medium of the Latin language, he might easily have obtained a complete knowledge of the discoveries of the Northmen—sufficient at least to confirm his belief in the existence of a Western continent. How much the discoveries of the distinguished Genoese navigator were exceeded by those of the Northmen, will appear from the following narratives." (Then follows the translation of the voyages so often referred to, the same that was published by the Prince Society, in Boston.)

"According to Irving's larger work," the same author remarks, "this visit (to Iceland) took place in February, 1477, when Columbus appears to have observed with surprise that the sea was not frozen. The learned Icelander, Finn Magnusen, directs attention to the following remarkable coincidence: 'In the year 1477, Magnus Eiolfson was Bishop of Skalholt in Iceland; since 1470 he had been abbot of the Monastery of Helgafell, the place where the oldest documents relating to Greenland, Vinland, and the various parts of America discovered by the Northmen had been written, and where they were doubtless carefully preserved, as it was from this very district that the most distinguished voyagers had gone forth. These documents must have been well known to Bishop Magnus, as were their general contents throughout the island, and it is, therefore, in the highest degree improbable that Columbus, whose mind had been filled with the idea of exploring a Western continent since the year 1474, should have omitted to seek for and receive information respecting these early voyages. He arrived at Hvalfjord, or Hvalfjardarejri, on the south coast of Iceland, at a time when that harbour was most frequented, and it is well known that Bishop Magnus visited the neighbouring churches in the spring or summer."

Laing gives still further information on this point, obtained from the same source and one other, namely, Captain Zahrtmann on the voyage of Zeno, and Finn Magnusen on "The English Trade to Iceland," second volume of "Nordisk Tidskrift," 1833. It is this: "Columbus came in spring to the south end of Iceland, where Whalefjord was the usual harbour, and it is known that Bishop Magnus, exactly in the spring of that year (1477), was on a visitation to that part of his see, and it is to be presumed Columbus must have met and conversed with him."

In a review of that great work by Professor Rafn, "Antiquitates Americanæ," which appeared in the *Foreign Quarterly Review*, for May, 1838, it is asked very aptly: "But what could be more to his purpose or better adapted to his views than the fact that the Northmen, the boldest of navigators, had knowledge of a land in the West which they supposed to extend far southwards till it met Africa? Or would not the intelligent Genoese find some suggestion in the following more accurate statement of an Icelandic geographer: '*On the west of the great sea of Spain*, which some call Ginnungagap, and leaning somewhat towards the north, the first land which occurs is the good Vinland?'"

If we turn to Swedish authors, we find the same belief with them, that Columbus paid a visit to Iceland and obtained there all the information requisite to enable him to carry out his presumptuous plan. Holmberg's words are conclusive: "With certainty do we know that Columbus toward the end of the fifteenth century, presumably in the year 1477, sojourned at Iceland, where he was sent by Englishmen, whose industrial mind had already fixed its attention upon Iceland's rich fisheries. Here he without doubt met the descendants of those who had first made said discovery, got knowledge of the written *sagor* thereof, and probably also obtained fresh intelligence concerning the great land in the West, *Vinland det goda*, as history is able to mention an American voyage only one hundred and thirty years previous. He was, however, sufficiently prudent never to reveal this, and such a trait perhaps diminishes his greatness. The edge of the well-known story of Columbus is through this turned against himself, and one cannot well avoid seeing a Nemesis in the fact that the New World did not obtain his name, but that of another who sailed in his wake."

And in Spain, when it became a matter of obtaining royal sanction to his enterprise, the funds to carry it through, what evidence so incontrovertible of the success that had attended his inquiries in Iceland as his supreme confidence—in himself?— no, in the *certainty* he had obtained up there in the North, from records that did not lie, like the Southern ones, from a people who did not lie, and who treasured the great deeds of their illustrious ancestors,—as his grand pretensions, and, for that matter, his patience and fortitude, which have been so much lauded, in holding out during so long a struggle and waiting? This *certainty*, based on reliable Icelandic records, was more stimulating than scientific knowledge, such scientific knowledge as he could command, more sustaining than faith, more delicious than even his own vanity! He was not too proud, this man, to enjoy a stolen inheritance.

As is well known, his plan stranded, in the first instance, on account of his preposterously high demands. Irving, observing the fact, but misconstruing the cause, says: "So fully imbued was Columbus with the grandeur of his enterprise, that he would listen to none but princely conditions." Not with "the grandeur of his enterprise," but with the money value of his stolen knowledge, the three-fold advantage of it to the Church, the throne of Spain and himself, was he imbued! "The courtiers who treated with him," continued Irving, "were indignant at such a demand. Their pride was shocked to see one whom they had considered as a needy adventurer, aspiring to rank and dignities superior to their own."

Needy adventurer he indeed was! But the consciousness that he had a genuine commodity for which he was sure to find a customer in the long run, gave him the hardihood to make large demands. Naturally insolent, this secret *certainty* inflated his insolence to the extreme of audacity. It was not reckless audacity, however, for he was sure of his ground, and could not very well presume too much.

The reader will now be interested to know what share of the spoils fell to Columbus—*these guaranteed beforehand*—as the result of the knowledge he stole at Iceland, and which rendered this trip the most successful voyage on record.

The following is quoted from Arthur Helps' "Life of Columbus:"—

"The favours which Christopher Columbus has asked from the King and Queen of Spain in recompense of the discoveries which he has made in the ocean seas, and as recompense for the voyage which he is about to undertake, are the following :—

"1. He wishes to be made admiral of the seas and countries which he is about to discover. He desires to hold this dignity during his life, and that it should descend to his heirs.

"*This request is granted by the King and Queen.*

"2. Christopher Columbus wishes to be made viceroy of all the continents and islands.

"*Granted by the King and Queen.*

"3. He wishes to have a share, amounting to a tenth part, of the profits of all merchandise, be it pearls, jewels, or any other things, that may be found, gained, bought, or exported from the countries which he is to discover.

"*Granted by the King and Queen.*

"4. He wishes, in his quality of admiral, to be made sole judge of all mercantile matters that may be the occasion of dispute in the countries which he is to discover.

"*Granted by the King and Queen on the condition that this jurisdiction should belong to the office of admiral as held by Don Enriques and other admirals.*

"5. Christopher Columbus wishes to have the right to contribute the eighth part of the expenses of all ships which traffic with the new countries, and in return to earn the eighth part of the profits.

"*Granted by the King and Queen.*

"Santa Fé, in the Vega of Granada,
"April 17th, 1492."

What share the Pope gave the King and Queen we already know!

REYKJAVIK HARBOUR.

CHAPTER VII.

THE SCANDINAVIAN NORTH AND SPAIN CONTRASTED.

THE signal national act of Spain, which has given it a ghastly preeminence—this act extended into a uniform line of conduct for several centuries—was that of crushing out all the civilization within its borders, or in lands adjacent to it. That which distinguishes ancient Scandinavia is its persistent resistance to the power that enabled Spain to do the European race this almost irreparable injury, the national traits of the Northern people alone preventing the injury from becoming universal destruction. To be sure, Llorente and others assert that Spain resisted the introduction of the Inquisition, "It is an incontestable fact," he says, "in the history of the Spanish Inquisition, that it was introduced entirely against the consent of the provinces, and only by the influence of the Dominican monks;" yet the resistance was but feeble, the ruling traits of the Spanish people, rightly defined by Buckle as loyalty and superstition, operating more decisively to further its introduction than even the zeal of the Dominicans. "These, then, were the two great elements of which the Spanish character was compounded. Loyalty and superstition; reverence for their kings and reverence for their clergy were the leading principles which influenced the Spanish mind, and governed the march of Spanish history," states Buckle succinctly. The popes and bishops of the fourth century had profited of the circumstance of the emperors having embraced Christianity, and this gave the Church the reins of power, while the predominant traits of the Spaniards rendered them submissive tools for any infamy Church and Throne united might devise. This nation were destitute of that instinct which was the strongest in the Norsemen, the instinct of freedom.

The motives for establishing the Inquisition must of necessity have actuated the Spaniards at large as well as the heads of the Church and the reigning sovereigns, Ferdinand and Isabella, else the people, weak as they were, could have frustrated the attempt of these to establish such a system of terrorism; but hatred of the Jews, a consuming envy of their superior prosperity, as well as their learning and skill, prevailed everywhere, and the ecclesiastical and imperial proposition to persecute this race in a body, met with a hearty response. Llorente declares this with absolute authority: "The Christians who could not rival them in industry, had almost all become their debtors, and envy soon made them the enemies of their creditors." The Spanish Moors were still more obnoxious to them. How could a race who were Christians in the full sense of the word, steeped in the ignorance and superstition that this implies, tolerate the proximity of a people whose "culture and prosperity rivalled the Golden Age of the Grecian Republics"? This glorious height had been reached, affirms Felix Oswald, two centuries after the conversion of Mecca, "and, six hundred years later, the Moors of Spain were still the teachers of Europe in science and arts, as well as in industry and in agriculture." True Christians are manifestly of the same type everywhere, and the Spanish Christians could not have differed essentially from the class in Greece and Rome upon which Celsus visits such severe reprobation. "You shall see weavers, tailors, fullers, and the most illiterate and rustic fellows, who dare not speak a word before wise men, when they can get a company of children and silly women together, set up to teach strange paradoxes among them. . . . This is one of their rules—Let no man that is learned, wise, or prudent come among us; but if any be unlearned, or a child, or an idiot, let him freely come. So they openly declare that none but fools and sots, and such as want sense, slaves, women and children, are fit disciples for the God they worship." St. Mark also, in the second chapter, sixteenth verse, says that Jesus went surrounded by men and women of ill-repute, and that the Pharisees and the learned were astonished that He ate and drank in such company. In a few terse words Felix Oswald draws the contrast between the enlightened and unenlightened in Spain: "At the same time when Moorish Spain rivalled the god-gardens of ancient Italy, and every Moorish town had its schools of poetry and philosophy, Christian Spain was cursed with a chronic plague of mental and physical famines." Prescott also affirms that "the Spanish Moors in the Peninsula reached a higher degree of civilization than in any other part of the world," and, furthermore, that "this period of brilliant illumination with the Saracens corresponds precisely with that of the deepest barbarism of Europe; when a library of three or four hundred volumes was a magnificent endowment for the richest monastery."

It was the same with the Albigenses, a refined, enlightened, free-minded people, opposed to the doctrines of Rome; they excited the same feelings of hatred, envy and malignity in the Spaniards, and the command to exterminate all three of these races, the Moors, Jews, and Albigenses, was more than welcome. This ready acceptance of a fiendish policy in itself proves Spain to have been brutally debased. In religious parlance this nation abhorred heresy; in the language of truth, it abhorred civilization. Nevertheless, it must be admitted candidly, that it is the only nation that has ever pursued a thoroughly consistent policy, for Christianity and civilization are utterly incompatible and cannot exist on the same soil. If salvation has any meaning, if faith is necessary for salvation, if heresy is a crime, entailing the most frightful consequences, here and hereafter, almost any means are justifiable to prevent that crime, and no means less rigorous than the Inquisition could have checked all the natural

I

instincts of the human heart and mind, the impulse, craving, determination, inseparable from human nature, for knowledge, freedom, happiness, progress, a natural and unrestrained life. If Christianity is better than all this, according to its own dogmatic assertion, which Spain implicitly believed, it was right to impose it there, through any means at command, which Spain did, and it would also be right to impose it, at this present day, on all the nations of the earth, and through the same means, the only effectual means, the Inquisition. Christianity, in short, pronounces human nature wrong, all its attributes wrong, and sets about a reconstruction so violent, so contrary to the mental, moral, and physical conformation of human beings, that nothing less than the extinction of the species will effect it. The Spanish Inquisition barely failed of this result within its own jurisdiction. Prescott sums up Llorente's figures thus: " Llorente computes that during the eighteen years of Torquemada's ministry, there were no less than 10,220 burnt, 6860 condemned and burnt in effigy as absent or dead, and 97,321 reconciled by various other penances; affording an average of more than 6000 convicted persons annually." But in his preface, this brave and outspoken man, who with almost superhuman courage dared to expose the full iniquity of the Inquisition, describes the evil it wrought: " I have also shown that these ministers of persecution have been the chief causes of the decline of literature, and almost the annihilators of nearly all that could enlighten the people, by their ignorance, their blind submission to the monks who were qualifiers, and by persecuting the magistrates and the learned who were anxious to disseminate information. These monks were despicable scholastic theologians, too ignorant and prejudiced to be able to ascertain the truth between the doctrines of Luther and those of Roman Catholicism, and so condemned as Lutheran, propositions incontestably true. The horrid conduct of this *holy office* weakened the power and diminished the population of Spain by arresting the progress of arts, sciences, industry, and commerce, and by compelling multitudes of families to abandon the kingdom, by instigating the expulsion of the Jews and the Moors, and by immolating on its flaming shambles more than *three hundred thousand victims ! !*"

Concerning this invaluable work, which will yet, I trust not in the far future, serve the purpose of doing away with Christianity as the prime cause, not only of this particular evil, but of all evil, Prescott writes: "Llorente's work well deserves to be studied as the record of the most humiliating triumph which fanaticism has ever been able to obtain over human reason, and that too during the most civilized periods and in the most civilized portion of the world." Llorente gives his own reasons for undertaking a work fraught with such difficulty and danger. "A firm conviction, from knowing the deep objects of this tribunal, that it was vicious in principle, in its constitution, and in its laws, notwithstanding all that has been said in its support, induced me to avail myself of the advantage my situation afforded me, and to collect every document I could procure relative to its history." He was secretary of the Inquisition at Madrid during the years 1789, 1790, and 1791.

The purpose was thus to exterminate heresy and heretics. Heresy, as we have seen, is a very comprehensive word, and in the effort to exterminate that, Spain was in reality exterminating all that was of value to the human race. In corroboration of this I quote several authors, for the testimony must be so abundant as to leave no doubt on this point. "It is remarkable that a scheme so monstrous as that of the Inquisition, presenting the most effectual barrier, probably, that was ever opposed to the progress of knowledge, should have been revived at the close of the fifteenth century, when the light of civilization was rapidly advancing over every part of Europe," writes Prescott, also remarking: "It is painful, after having dwelt so long on the important benefits resulting to Castile from the comprehensive policy of Isabella,[1] to be compelled to turn to the darker side of the picture, and to exhibit her as accommodating herself to the illiberal spirit of the age in which she lived, so far as to sanction one of the grossest abuses that ever disgraced humanity." Buckle's verdict is this: "In such a state of society, anything approaching to a secular or scientific spirit was, of course, impossible. Every one believed; no one inquired. Among the better classes, all were engaged in war or theology, and most were occupied with both. Those who made literature a profession, ministered, as professional men too often do, to the prevailing prejudice. . . . The quantity of Spanish works to prove the necessity of religious persecution is incalculable; and this took place in a country where not one man in a thousand doubted the propriety of burning heretics. . . . The greatest men, with hardly an exception, became ecclesiastics, and all temporal considerations, all views of earthly policy, were despised and set at naught. No one inquired; no one doubted; no one presumed to ask if all this was right. The minds of men succumbed and were prostrate. While every other country was advancing, Spain alone was receding. Every other country was making some addition to knowledge, creating some art, or enlarging some science. Spain, numbed into a deathlike torpor, spell-bound and entranced by the accursed superstition which preyed on her strength, presented to Europe a solitary instance of constant decay." There were other practical results to which he also draws attention: "The Spanish Christians considered agriculture beneath their dignity. In their judgment war and religion were the only two avocations worthy of being followed. Some of the richest parts of Valencia and Granada were so neglected that means were wanting to feed even the scanty population remaining there. Whole districts were deserted, and down to the present day have never been repeopled. All over Spain

---

[1] "History of the Reign of Ferdinand and Isabella," W. H. Prescott.

the same destitution prevailed. That once rich and prosperous country was covered with a rabble of monks and clergy, whose insatiate rapacity absorbed the little wealth yet to be found. The fields were left uncultivated; vast multitudes died from want and exposure; entire villages were deserted."

W. H. Lecky, in his "History of Rationalism," describes another phase of the evil: "The persecutor can never be certain that he is not persecuting truth rather than error, but he may be quite certain that he is suppressing the spirit of truth. And indeed, it is no exaggeration to say that the doctrines I have reviewed represent the most skilful and at the same time most successful conspiracy against that spirit that has ever existed among mankind. Until the seventeenth century, every mental disposition which philosophy pronounces to be essential to a legitimate research was almost uniformly branded as a sin; and a large proportion of the most deadly intellectual vices were deliberately inculcated as virtues. . . . In a word, there is scarcely a disposition that marks the love of abstract truth, and scarcely a rule which reason teaches as essential for its attainment, that theologians did not for centuries stigmatize as offensive to the Almighty."

Felix Oswald groups the evils thus: "Hence, inquisitions and crusades, thirty years' wars, heretic-hunts, massacres of S.. Bartholomew, expulsions of the Moors, and exterminations of the Albigenses." He asks: "Has the happiness of the human race been secured, or in any degree promoted, by the dogmas of the Christian religion?" And then proceeds to say the words which the continued presence of Roman Catholicism, or original Christianity, in the midst of civilized modern communities, renders so imperatively necessary: "Cowardice and stupidity have too long connived at the crime of abetting the dissemination of that earth-blighting superstition, and it is time to say the truth in plain terms. The demonstrable truth then is that, if all the countries of Europe that were destined to pass under the yoke of the Cross had, instead, for a thousand years been covered by the ashes of the fire-storm that buried the cities of Pompeii and Herculaneum, the world would to-day be benefited by the result. Our earth would be more fertile and prosperous, our fellow-men would be freer, wiser, and happier. The waste of the volcanic cinders would have proved less irreclaimable than the desert of pessimism. The survivors of the catastrophe would have saved their children from the alternative of death or moral slavery that awaited the next forty generations of their descendants. The nations of the Caucasian race would have been spared the systematic extirpation of their wisest and bravest men. The Saracens, whose Western empire was destroyed by the insane fanaticism of the Christian priests, would have cultivated the garden of civilization in a more grateful soil."

Llorente states as a fact that "the war against the Albigenses was the first cause of the establishment of the Inquisition, and the pretended necessity of punishing the apostacy of the newly-converted Spanish Jews was the reason for introducing it in a reformed state." After a very thorough dissection of all the motives and objects, he says: "It is to these projects"—having proved most of them to be *mercenary*—"concealed under the appearance of zeal for religion, that the Inquisition of Spain owes its origin." Prescott also says that "some writers are inclined to show the Spanish Inquisition, in its origin, as little else than a political engine," and throws further light on the motives of the Pope that instigated it: "Sixtus IV., who at that time filled the pontifical chair, easily discerning the sources of wealth and influence which this measure opened to the Court of Rome, readily complied with the petition of the sovereigns, and expedited a bull bearing date November 1st, 1478, authorizing them to appoint two or three ecclesiastics inquisitors for the detection and suppression of heresy throughout their dominions." But it is reserved for Llorente to state this with full authority and reveal the ferocious brigandage of the Church officials: "Facts prove beyond a doubt," he says, "that the extirpation of Judaism was not the real cause, but the mere pretext, for the establishment of the Inquisition by Ferdinand V. The true motive was to carry on a vigorous system of confiscation against the Jews, and so bring their riches into the hands of the Government. Sixtus IV. sanctioned the measure to gain the point dearest to the Court of Rome, an extent of domination." In revealing the intricate mechanism of the Inquisition, its invisible network, its secrecy, its diabolical craft and artifice, he shows how impossible it was for a victim to escape from its toils, except by a deeper cunning than the inquisitors themselves were masters of, for "the Inquisition employed every means and neglected nothing in the trials of the prisoners to make them appear guilty of heresy, and all this was done with an appearance of charity and compassion, and in the name of Jesus Christ." Prescott, too, remarks: "The sword of justice was observed, in particular, to strike at the wealthy, the least pardonable offenders in time of proscription."

This strips away the last disguise; whatever religious zeal, bigotry, or fanaticism may have fired the uninitiated, the heads of the Church at Rome were actuated by money-greed and love of dominion; this also removes the last excuse of those religious persons everywhere, who are always ready to extenuate the crimes of the Church and to find justification for all forms of intolerance. The Inquisition was highway robbery and murder on a stupendous scale. If missionary work of all kinds, conversion, and proselyting is less than that in our own day, it is only because the moment is not propitious for the full operation of the system, the Church not being in a position to employ all its resources. No other nation than Spain has ever allowed it to exercise its full prerogative.

This privilege extended over a considerable length of time, as Llorente shows: "Charles V. protected it (the Inquisition) from motives of policy, being convinced it was the only means of preventing the heresy of Luther from penetrating into Spain. Philip II. was actuated by superstition and tyranny to uphold it; and even extended its jurisdiction to the excise, and made the exporters of horses into France liable to seizure by the officers of the tribunal, as persons suspected of heresy. Philip III., Philip IV., and Charles II. pursued the same course, stimulated by similar fanaticism and imbecility, when the reunion of Portugal to Spain led to the discovery of many Jews. Philip V. maintained the Inquisition from considerations of mistaken policy, inherited from Louis XIV., who made him believe that such rigour would ensure the tranquillity of the kingdom, which was always in danger when many religions were tolerated. Ferdinand VI. and Charles III. befriended this holy office, because they would not deviate from the course that their father had traced, and because the latter hated the freemasons. Lastly, Charles IV. supported the tribunal, because the French Revolution seemed to justify a system of surveillance, and he found a firm support in the zeal of the inquisitors-general, always attentive to the preservation and extension of their power, as if the sovereign authority could find no surer means of strengthening the throne than the terror inspired by an Inquisition."

The Inquisition has continued into the present century. The Spaniards made an abortive attempt to abolish it in 1820, and we learn that it was mitigated in 1834; it can almost be regarded throughout as a modern institution, Spain's defence against the encroachment of enlightenment through the Moors, the Jews, the Albigenses, French infidelity, and Lutheranism! It is not so very long since this paragraph appeared in a New York paper: "What is the matter with Spain? She seems to be utterly dull, lifeless, and inert. Germany, France, and Italy are pressing on grandly towards liberal and representative government, sloughing the gangrene of vicious political practices, and breaking down the barriers reared by the enemies of the people. Everywhere within their boundaries is life and activity, mental and physical."

Spain's hope for the future has manifestly lain in the characteristic effort to gain spiritual ascendency in the United States through foisting upon the young and *rich* Republic, as discoverer, saint, paragon, claimant-in-chief for American gratitude, the Italian fanatic and charlatan, Christopher Columbus! In its folly and infatuation, Spain no doubt looks forward to the re-establishment of the Inquisition on American soil, where the opportunities for persecution and confiscation would be more brilliant even than in Spain, when three races were extirpated!

With what sickening disgust and loathing one turns from this black picture, from the nation which, in alliance with Rome, blighted the race! But if Spain, past or present, is the most horrible subject in Europe to survey, the North is the brightest! Spain blighted, the North saved! Spain exhibits deformity, the North the natural man; one of the finest types the earth has produced, in some attributes excelling all others. Spain, in devotion to its religion, laboured for the extinction of manhood; the Northern nations, whether inside or outside of their religion, worshipped manhood, and cultivated it to a high degree of perfection in themselves. In this they resembled the Greeks, but were even more rigid in conforming to their own standard of excellence, tolerating no defect or weakness in themselves. Whatever they did was in obedience to the requirements of their ideal. And this was not from any species of fear; the hell of their religion, if anything of so slight religious substance can be called a religion, was for those who felt fear, for *cowards;* there these most despicable of wretches were consigned to a Palace of Anguish, had Famine for their board, Slowness and Delay for their attendants, and slept on a Bed of Care; and this is so purely retributive justice that no thinking person can deplore it. Their hell would be filled with the elect of the Christian world, and Spain, with its two distinguishing national traits, "loyalty and superstition," would go there *en masse*, together with the hordes of zealots it has propagated in other lands, and in its possessions in South America. If the Norsemen worshipped Odin and Thor, it was because they considered them good, brave, intelligent fellows, worthy of admiration, and not because servile adoration was obligatory upon them; if any doubted the virtues or superior excellence of these gods, they did not hesitate to say so, and did not profess to revere them unless this was their sincere feeling. "The Inquisition," according to Llorente, "encouraged hypocrisy, and punished those who either did not know how to, or would not, assume the mask." Christianity in itself encouraged hypocrisy; but hypocrisy was the vice that the Odin-worshippers, so-called, considered most despicable; they were as free from that as the Spaniards were from sincerity. We are all of us, at this present day, chiefly indebted to Spain and to Rome for what Felix Oswald calls "that chief disgrace of our own age—the cowardly hypocrisy which, like an all-pervading poison-vapour, taints the whole atmosphere of our social life."

A mythological religion did not satisfy the Northern mind, however grand the mythology and exalted its personages, although the Southern mind could thrive for centuries on "Buddhism and its daughter-creed," as Oswald rightly designates the Christian myth, adding that these "can flourish only in a sickly soil. Christianity developed its first germs in the carcass of the decaying Roman Empire, and still retains its firmest hold upon the degenerate nations of Southern Europe; while the manlier races of the North resisted its propaganda to the last, and were the first to free themselves from its despotism." A. E. Holmberg notes this absence of the spirit of idolatry in the Scandinavians:" Without doubt this lack (in the Asa-doctrine) of a rational morality, conduced with more thoughtful minds to bring it into contempt. We find, namely, as far as that is concerned, very prevalent free-thinking, which directed itself now to something better, now to something worse, as well as a consequent tolerance toward those who thought differently, which, however, declined toward the close of that doctrine's life."

That the Norsemen took their divinities entirely on their merits is proven by a multitude of anecdotes from those times, and that they were not allowed to subject Jesus Christ to the same criticism must have been a most surprising after-revelation to them! The following stories are narrated by Mallet, in his "Northern Antiquities:" "In the history of Olaf Tryggveson a warrior fears not to say publicly that he relies much more on his own strength and on his arms, than upon Thor or Odin. Another, in the same book, speaks thus to his friend: 'I would have thee know that I believe neither in idols nor spirits. I have travelled in many places; I have met with giants and monstrous men: they could never overcome me; thus to this present hour my own force and courage are the sole objects of my belief.' ... In an Icelandic chronicle a vain-glorious man makes his boast to a Christian missionary that he had never yet acknowledged any religion, and that his own strength and abilities were everything to him. For the same reason others refused to sacrifice to the gods of whom they had no need. ... In the life of King Olaf Tryggveson, mention is made of a man who was condemned to exile for having sung in a public place, verses the sense of which was to this purpose, 'I will not insult or affront the gods; nevertheless the goddess Freja inspires me with no respect: it must certainly be that either she or Odin are chimerical deities.'"

Free to think and act, to follow their impulses, the dearest aim of the Norsemen was to cultivate character, to attain that degree of excellence which would make their life a joy to them; their heaven was only valuable to them as following upon a valuable life here on earth, and they were never disposed to resign this life for the sake of a future one; if they sought death, or met it bravely, it was for other reasons, not savouring of sickly renunciation. This aim of theirs to be great, developed a heroic age; the warriors and the bards emulated each other, one to supply valorous deeds, worthy of being eulogized in inspired improvization, the other to praise these deeds as they deserved, and transmit the memory of them to posterity. The court was the scene of this laurel-crowning, and the king, the comrade of the warriors, not an isolated despot enjoining homage and plotting ruin for his subjects, was a fellow-aspirant for these honours, gaining his glory on the same high path. So much were the bards respected, that one of these, though a stranger, needed no introduction at court. P. E. Müller, who is one of the most reliable of authors on this subject, asserts that "no nation ever possessed a poetry more strictly national than the Scandinavian." This was due to the fact that the individuals of the nation possessed character, that their actions and thoughts were spontaneous, allowing free play to their genius, which in its turn, feeling no curb or restriction, engendered a boundless ambition and love of fame. "Harold Hårfager's reign," says Müller, "was the Augustan age of the Scalds. Ambitious and warlike, he kept a splendid court, to which he sought to draw all the distinguished men of his country." The advent of Christianity changed things in this respect. The same author continues: "Olaf Tryggveson's zeal for Christianity caused him rather to discourage than to favour the Scalds; but one of them, indignant at seeing his art slighted, forced the king to listen to his song, by declaring that if he did not, he would immediately abjure Christianity, which Olaf, with much trouble, had induced him to embrace." Some other words of Müller's bear upon the point I have drawn attention to, the cultivation of character among the Norsemen, an object which the Christians have uniformly neglected out of contempt for their own nature, and human nature in general, and the other members of the community, in modern times, passive Christians for the most part, wearing the badge, but evading the observances, have set aside, for the reason that the pursuit of knowledge or wealth was more agreeable to them, requiring one or other of these to stimulate pride in themselves or even self-respect. The modern man, as a rule, has no very great respect for character in the abstract, does not believe in it, in fact; he believes that men are made by their circumstances, not that truth, courage, sincerity, goodness, have the slightest power in and of themselves, or that these mould circumstances. Here we see the blessed fruits of the Spanish Inquisition. The stigma still attached to heresy, heterodox views or freethought, is another.

The words of Müller referred to are these: "The importance attached by the Scandinavians to the delineation of character is evident from the language itself, which is much richer than any other of Europe in all terms expressive of characteristic qualities, whether of mind or body, so as to be able to convey the strength, weakness, obstinacy, quarrelsome or peaceable disposition of every individual in its finest shades." The vocation of Scald, therefore, was one that required the nicest discrimination and power of analysis, as well as rhetorical skill, and as absolute truthfulness was demanded both by the subject of the epic, if he happened to be present, and the assembled hearers, this could only be gained by accuracy of perception, the same exactness in delineating traits of character, all that pertains to one individuality as distinct from another, as an artist must use in portraying features that are to be a true likeness of the sitter. As knowledge of character could only be attained through knowledge of the world, and as the characters to be drawn, far from being simple, provincial ones, of a settled type, were complex, finely-organized ones, developed through the largest intercourse with foreign nations, none but the most accomplished men of the world were competent to undertake the task of making that first oral record of their attributes, personality, and deeds that was to be preserved and transmitted as history. That the narratives from these times which claim to be historical, as distinct from fabulous, romantic, or mythological, are uniformly vouched for, by the best authorities of the present day, as authentic and reliable, is due to the correctness of the first analysis and description of the Scalds, the eye-witnesses, and keen, incorruptible judges of the events and persons they described. One could almost venture to say that this in itself renders ancient Scandinavian history more valuable and trustworthy than any other. After the introduction of Christianity not even a Scald of the North could dare to "speak the truth, the whole truth, and nothing but the truth!" That which a Spanish writer says of the Moors: "Their trustworthiness was such, that their bare word was more relied on than a written contract is now among us," and the rules of life laid down in Hávamál: "A man ought to be self-reliant, wise, prudent, mild, hospitable, temperate, firm in friendship, magnanimous toward the weak and those seeking protection, inflexible in his promises and faithful in his obligations," were only possible among those who were un-Christianized.

Consequently the Scalds travelled abroad, going from court to court, not only for fame and profit, but to perfect themselves in their high calling, to learn to see with their own eyes and to judge with their own understanding; such was their ability to form an opinion of their own and to rely on it, that it is doubtful whether they would have read columns upon columns in the newspapers to know what was generally thought of such and such a hero, general, king, or leader, even if newspapers had been at their command, and no instance is recorded of a Scald going to a secret group of other Scalds to get their opinion of some high person before he committed himself to an open avowal. Much as they worshipped fame, theirs was not the name-worship and label-worship of the present day, an utter inability to value the work, or the production, or the deed, until they knew the name of the well established celebrity who could claim the honour of it. Fame was of that summer's growth, was plucked ripe from the branch, fresh fruit for fresh young lips, and no aspirant was kept waiting. If the hero was a boy, a mere stripling, he enjoyed the same honour as if a grey-haired man, in fact more; the Norsemen were not over fond of senility, and for a man to outlive his usefulness was a great reproach. Whatever fame a man was deserving of he received, and received quickly; the Scald apparently was such a personification of just criticism as modern civilization has not been blessed with.

In Laing's preliminary dissertation to the "Heimskringla," there is much said in their praise: "From their opportunities of visiting various countries, the Icelandic Scalds were undoubtedly the educated men of the times when books did not in any way contribute to intelligence, or to forming the mind; but only extensive intercourse with men, and the information gathered from it.... They had also the advantage of speaking in its greatest purity what was the court language in Norway, Sweden, Denmark, England, and at Rouen." Grenville Pigott adds another fact in regard to them: "It was not therefore until some time after the race of Scalds was extinct in the three great Scandinavian kingdoms, that those of Iceland attained their highest perfection. Their fame spread abroad, and the successful examples of Eigil Skalagrimson and of some others, encouraged them to perfect themselves, and to travel from court to court in search of fame and profit. We accordingly hear of them in the courts of England, Ireland, Scotland, Norway, Sweden, Denmark, the courts of the Orkneys, and in various other places."

But if the Scald was a good critic, he was also in presence of a good critic in the person of the king he extolled, the practical hero, as a rule, being possessed of what we consider, in this age, the impractical part of a man's equipment for the world, intellectual gifts. The kings and heroes were not infrequently Scalds themselves, just as the Scalds were very often tried warriors. "The famous king Ragnar Lodbrok, his queen Aslög or Aslauga, and his adventurous sons, who distinguished themselves by their maritime incursions into England and France in the ninth century, were all Scalds," as Wheaton informs us, and Mallet says: "In a word, the poetic art was held in such high estimation, that great lords and even kings did not disdain to cultivate it with the utmost pains themselves." As for the kings, two of them at least, Thomas Carlyle has a highly characteristic word to say about them: "Remarkable old men, these two first kings" (Harold Hårfager and Gorm the Old); "and possessed of gifts for bringing Chaos a little nearer to the form of Cosmos; possessed, in fact, of loyalties to Cosmos, that is to say, of authentic virtues in the savage state, such as have been needed in all societies at their incipience in this world; a kind of 'virtues' hugely in discredit at present, but not unlikely to be needed again, to the astonishment of careless persons, before all is done!"

And the courts? It would seem that these were not unworthy of the Scalds. Pigott says: "The courts of the first Dukes of Normandy, composed exclusively of the descendants of the Scandinavian conquerors of Neustria, and continually recruited from their kinsmen in the North, were the most polished and chivalrous of the time; and it is notorious that the chiefs who accompanied William to the Conquest of England, looked upon the uncouth manners of the Anglo-Saxon nobles with undisguised contempt." He also recalls the fact that "the great traveller, Pythias, who lived about the time of Alexander the Great, and later, Tacitus, described the Scandinavians as superior in civilization to the Celts and Germans." "Their royal house," says Adam of Bremen, speaking of the Swedes, "is very ancient; but the king's power depends on the voice of the people." Müller, as we have seen, compares Harold Hårfager's reign to the Augustan age.

The courts, then, were the hotbeds of Scandinavian literature and history, and the Scalds were the gardeners. It now behoves us to consider the quality of this literature. That it is reliable, historically, is its highest excellence, particularly now when history has been proven such treacherous ground; " Prof. Müller shows," says Pigott, " that the greater portion of the early Sagas may be depended upon as faithful historical narratives." Wilhelmi, in his " Discovery of America by the Northmen, 500 years before Columbus," goes still further, and declares that the Eddas and the old Norse sagor, and not Cæsar, Tacitus, Procopius, Jornandes, Paulus Diaconus, Adam of Bremen, and the rest, were the especial sources of knowledge of the religious doctrines of the Germans. In the "'Heimskringla,'" he says, "we obtain from the narratives of the Icelanders' extensive journeys through all Europe to Rome, Constantinople, and Jerusalem, also the knowledge of the history, geography and antiquity of eastern, western and southern Europe." So these were no local annals of a single obscure race! In regard to the extent of this literature, Laing contributes some valuable information: "The following list will show the reader"—one taken from that given by Thormod Torfaeus, in his "Series Dynastarum et Regum Daniæ," from that given by Müller, in his " Saga-bibliothek," and from that of Biorn Haldorson—"that in the five centuries between the days of the venerable Bede and those of Matthew Paris, that is from the ninth to the end of the thirteenth century, the northern branch of the common race was not destitute of intellectuality, notwithstanding all their paganism and barbarism, and had a literature adapted to their national spirit, and wonderfully extensive." In this list of 169 works, forty-eight are historical, and forty-six works of fiction, while the remainder are mixed fable and history, poetical or mythological works. Besides these, there are other works cited by the ancient historians. "Scarcely any of it," observes Laing, "consists of the legends of saints, or homilies, or theological treatises, which constitute the greater proportion of the literature of other countries during the same ages, and which were evidently composed only for the public of the cloisters." An eminent American author, Hubert Howe Bancroft, expresses an opinion concerning European literature, during this and a later period, that coincides perfectly with the statement here given: "Learning, such as it was, had hitherto been almost the exclusive property of the Church, which vehemently repudiated science as absolutely incompatible with its pretensions; now and then gleams of important truths would flash up in the writings of some heretical philosopher, illuminating for a moment the path of intellectual progress; but such dangerous fires were speedily quenched, and that they might not spring forth again to endanger the religious equilibrium of Christendom, their authors were generally destroyed. The literature of the age consisted for the most part of musty manuscripts, emanating from musty minds, utterly devoid of thought and destitute of reason."

After dwelling on the peculiar quality of mind, and the prowess of the Scandinavians, Laing continues: "It will not at least surprise the philosophic reader that some of this mental power was applied at home in attempts, however rude, at history and poetry; but he will be surprised to find that those attempts surpass, both in quality and quantity, all that can be produced in Anglo Saxon literature during the same ages, either in the Anglo-Saxon language or in the Latin." In regard to Snorre Sturleson's "Chronicles of the Kings of Norway," he says: "His work stands unrivalled in the Middle Ages. In that class of literary production—the lively representation of historical events by incidents, anecdotes, speeches, touches true to nature, bringing out strongly the character and individuality of each eminent actor in historical events—it may be doubted if, even since the

Middle Ages, any, excepting Shakespeare and Sir Walter Scott in their historical representations, have surpassed Snorre Sturleson."

Wheaton offers further evidence of the concurrence of authors in respect to the merits of ancient Scandinavian literature: "In Iceland an independent literature grew up, flourished, and was brought to a certain degree of perfection, before the revival of learning in the south of Europe. This island was not converted to Christianity until the end of the tenth century, when the national literature, which still remained in oral tradition, was full-blown and ready to be committed to a written form. With the Romish religion, Latin letters were introduced; but instead of being used, as elsewhere, to write a dead language, they were adapted by the learned men of Iceland to mark the sounds which had been before expressed by the Runic characters." His words *"the revival of learning in the south of Europe,"* bring to one's mind the *extinction* of learning there, incident upon the introduction of "the blessed light of Christianity," as it is rapturously styled. It is hard to believe that the following was ever true of the country where Christianity was allowed to shed its *full* effulgence and germinate its peculiar products: "Spain, a provincial part of Arabian dominion, was especially the seat of Arabian learning. Cordova, Granada, Seville, and all the cities of the peninsula, rivalled each other in the magnificence of their schools, academies, colleges, and libraries." And what were the effects of that enlightened and beneficent faith upon literature and learning? Llorente states: "Since the establishment of the holy office, there has scarcely been any man celebrated for his learning, who has not been prosecuted as a heretic;" and he gives a most appalling list of the victims among savants and literati, besides describing many of the trials and *autos-da-fé*. "The theological censures," he says, "likewise attack works on philosophy, on civil and natural law, and on the people. Those books which have been published on mathematics, astronomy, physic and other subjects which depend upon these, have not been more highly favoured. The Spaniards have, consequently, been deprived of the advantages which other nations have derived from all the recent discoveries."

No wonder then, knowing the "*holy office*" as he did, that he was amazed at what he experienced in England! I quote his own words: "*During the time I remained in London, I heard some Catholics affirm that the Inquisition was useful in Spain, to preserve the Catholic faith, and that a similar institution would have been useful in France.*"

How extraordinary, in the face of these execrable facts, of the chronology of horrors designated as the Middle Ages— it is a strange coincidence that the black death was brought from Palestine to Apulia and raged from 1347 to 1351—of the woe and desolation, the brutal ignorance and diabolism that reigned supreme, and were the immediate results of the establishment of Christianity (the edict of the Emperor Theodius against the Manicheans, in 382, being the virtual origin of the Inquisition, for, as Llorente states, " it is here that inquisition and accusation are first mentioned in relation to heresy ")—how extraordinary, I repeat, that any authors, outside of the priesthood, can attribute all the *good* that has befallen the race to this accursed idolatry! Even so intelligent an author as Mallet, after expressing the highest admiration of the Scandinavians, and mentioning especially those traits of character which were the direct antitheses of Christian traits, as impossible in a Christian convert as a lighted torch in a ditch,—writes such sickening twaddle as this: " Such was the immediate effect of Christianity in the north, an event which, considered only in a philosophical light, should be ever regarded as the dawn of those happy days which were afterwards to shine out with superior splendour. In effect, this religion, which tended to correct the abuse of licentious liberty, to banish bloody dissensions from among individuals, to restrain robberies and piracy, softening the ferocity of manners, requiring a certain knowledge of letters and history, re-establishing a part of mankind, who groaned under a miserable slavery, in their natural rights, introducing a relish for a life of peace, and an idea of happiness independent of sensual gratifications, sowed the seeds, if I may so speak, of that new spirit which grew to maturity in the succeeding ages, and to which the arts and sciences, springing up along with it, added still more strength and vigour." Could a greater satire be found than this upon the actual conditions resulting from Christianity? It is a work of supererogation to single out particular phrases, such as "the dawn of those happy days," "to correct the abuse of licentious liberty," "to banish bloody dissensions," "to restrain robberies and piracy," "requiring a certain knowledge of letters and history," &c., as specimens of exquisite, although unconscious, irony; it will suffice to blot out this pernicious nonsense with one sharp sentence of Felix Oswald's: "The warriors of the old pagan Northland, with all their martial truculence, would have shuddered at the mention of the inhumanities which their children perpetrated at the instigation of their priests." No, "the dawn of those happy days" actually culminated in this: "At the end of the thirteenth century, the enemies of nature had reached the zenith of their power; and, at that time, it may be said that *without a single exception*, the countries of Christian Europe were worse governed, more ignorant, more superstitious, poorer, and unhappier than the worse governed province of pagan Rome." This is Oswald's assertion again, and is absolutely true.

This anti-naturalism, alas! also fastened itself upon the North. The Norse nature, fortunately, was not as receptive to the poison as the Spanish, in fact, was not receptive to it at all; the Scandinavians did not accept Christianity voluntarily, but they were deceived and forced into the acceptance of it, *not knowing what it was*. Although intellectual beings, shrewd and sagacious, they had nothing in their mental endowment that could imagine or fathom the hellish craft and ingenuity of the Roman Catholics; neither their moral nor spiritual experience could enable them to anticipate what this new religion really was, or would do to them. In Spain, on the other hand, it was almost indigenous. Once there, however, in the North, it could not fail to have its customary effect, differing only in intensity, inasmuch as the innate freedom of the Northern mind could never cease to battle with the insidious oppressor. Thanks to this resistance, "the churchmen were not a numerous or powerful class until after the first half of the twelfth century; they were at first strangers, and many of them English." And thanks to this same resistance, Bishop Brask, who tried to introduce the Inquisition in Sweden, early in the sixteenth century, failed in the attempt. The writings of the very first Icelander who began to transcribe the history of the North, or to reproduce the *Sagor*, betrayed the Christian touch. This man was Are hinn Frode, whose work dates from about 1120. He was a priest. Concerning his production, Wheaton says: "His work, the 'Landnamma-Bok,' is therefore to be considered rather as a chronicle of the Christian Middle Ages than a child of the Northern muse. But his talents as an historian are incomparably superior to his monkish contemporaries on the Continent. He always writes with the good sense and the manly freedom of a citizen and a patriot, unaffected with that grovelling spirit of superstition which then darkened the face of Europe." His annals extend from the latter part of the ninth century to the beginning of the twelfth.

Fortunately the Sagor had been composed before; to collect and transcribe these was the principal duty of the early writers, and their patriotism, conscientiousness, and habitual truthfulness, led them to do this faithfully. The old material was sedulously collected and put into permanent shape, but the Christian religion soon deprived them of new, by changing the spirit of the age. This is shown inferentially by the following paragraph from Pigott's "Scandinavian Mythology:" "In the year 1262 Iceland was united to the crown of Norway. By this revolution it was indeed freed from the miseries brought upon it by its turbulent chiefs; but all interest in public affairs thenceforth died away, and no Sagas were written, because there was nothing to write about. They were replaced by dry chronicles, which also ceased with the great plague in 1350, and were not resumed until so late as the seventeenth century."

Still the darkness did not settle down upon the North as upon the rest of Europe, and but a few years ago Wilhelmi could exclaim: "Iceland's old glory has not yet disappeared, but reminds one, on the contrary, of the scientific life, which still develops itself there, of the brilliant antiquity, when this remote island, in the neighbourhood of the North Pole, was, in a scientific respect, *one of the brightest points on earth.*"

And, indeed, how could it fail to be; how could all Scandinavia fail to be one of the brightest points on earth, with such people as are described in the following paragraph? And by a foreigner, too, quoted in the first part of "Sveriges Historia:" "A stranger, who in an unusually high degree made himself familiar with the condition in the North during the time that is now in question, says of the Norsemen and their life during the last century of paganism: 'The stress that was laid upon intercourse with other persons, and the love for joyous festivals, woman's free and respected position, as well as the profound understanding of her relation to man, which is not seldom expressed in the *Sagor*, the high value that was assigned to the poetic art and all attainments, the zeal with which one, through travel in foreign countries, sought to acquire knowledge, together with many other traits in the ancient Northern folk-life, show, that one did not only take life from the dismal and rude side, and that we must not by any means imagine the Scandinavian pagans to be such savage and insensible barbarians as

they are usually described by their English and French enemies.'"
In physical attributes these Northerners were also conspicuous
and compelled the admiration of their foes. A. E. Holmberg
states that "the foreign annalists, who have had an opportunity
to take closer cognizance of the Northmen who overran Europe
during the Viking expeditions, coincide therein, that they have
never seen handsomer or taller men than these robbers, at the
same time that they praise their strength and bravery and also
such traits of character as keeping their word and the like."

It was no ferocious and bloodthirsty impulse that led them
into warfare; they made war because this was to them the path
of glory. Their religion, so to speak, enforced bravery, just as
the Christian doctrine enforced cowardice. Thomas Carlyle
describes it well, when he says: "That Norse religion, a rude
but earnest, sternly impressive *Consecration of Valour* (so we may
define it) sufficed for these old valiant Norsemen." And did
the Christians then never fight, never wage war, never shed
blood, that they denounce all this so fiercely in the Norsemen?
And which were the nobler, wars, or crusades, for the extermination of heretics, or wars of conquest over depraved and
enfeebled Catholic nations for the purpose of founding better
nations on the ruins of the old, of establishing free institutions and manly customs? Was an instance ever known of
the Scandinavians making a nation worse than they found it?
Their incursions were a severe remedy, to be sure, but has the
thinking world ever considered how things would have been if
the Vikings had never made any expeditions, but had remained
quietly at home, allowing the swarms of black-gowned priests
to rule the whole of Europe with the crucifix and to settle its
fate for all time? And when we Americans owe what we value
most in life to the grand Norse conquests, why should we be
loth to ascribe the same glory to these ancient conquerors as to
Napoleon or any other modern general?

To be sure, they did not parade their intentions in the way of national reform and republican organizations, but after their conquests the result was invariably the same, the work of reconstruction was begun at once, and all Europe was, in fact, remodelled by them. Mallet does them full justice in the following description: "In effect, we everywhere see in those swarms of Germans and Scandinavians, a troop of savage warriors, who seem only born for ravage and destruction, changed into a sensible and free people as soon as ever they had confirmed their conquests; impregnating (if I may so say) their institutions with a spirit of order and equality; electing for their kings such of their princes of the blood royal as they judged most worthy to wear the crown; dividing between those kings and the whole nation the exercise of the sovereign power; reserving to the general assemblies the right of making laws and deciding important matters; and lastly, to give a solid support to the powers immediately essential to monarchy, distributing fiefs to the principal warriors, and assigning certain privileges proper to the several orders of the state."

Warfare, too, aside from its martial or political bearing, was their chosen method for the perfecting of character, absolute courage being the finishing touch. They fought joyously, jubilantly, and met death with a laugh. "Accordingly," says Mallet, "we never find any among these people guilty of cowardice, and the bare suspicion of that vice was always attended with universal contempt. . . . Lastly, like the heroes of Homer, those of ancient Scandinavia, in the excess of their over-boiling courage, dared to defy the gods themselves. 'Though they should be stronger than the gods,' says a boastful warrior, speaking of his enemies, 'I would absolutely fight them.'"

But these people were much else besides warriors, were as remarkable for their versatility as for their surpassing ability in certain directions. Thus Laing observes: "In the characters of great men given in the sagas we always find eloquence, ready, agreeable speaking, a good voice, a quick apprehension, a ready delivery, and winning manners, reckoned the highest qualities of a popular king or eminent chief. His talent as a public speaker is never omitted." And Prof. R. B. Anderson, too, exclaims: "Yes; the Norsemen were truly a great people! Their spirit found its way into the Magna Charta of England and into the Declaration of Independence in America. The spirit of the Vikings still survives in the bosoms of Englishmen, Americans, and Norsemen, extending their commerce, taking bold positions against tyranny, and producing wonderful internal improvements in these countries."

In the Norsemen one continually has the gratifying surprise of hearing of a race who, in all the main political and social questions, were right in themselves, without the need of reform or agitation. That the people, in Scandinavia, had a voice in public affairs, is best proven by the fact that the people of America and England are free, at least comparatively so, in a political respect. Laing says of this: "Our civil, religious, and political rights,—the principles, spirit, and forms of legislation through which they work in our social union, are the legitimate offspring of the Things of the Northmen, not of the Wittenagemoth of the Anglo-Saxons—of the independent Norse Viking, not of the abject Saxon monk."

But nothing gives such conclusive evidence that our present state of civilization is not the outgrowth of a steady progressive development from the earliest ages, but is the feeble revival of a civilization, ripe, far advanced, brilliant, that was destroyed at the beginning of the Middle Ages,—as the position that woman held in the North. "In pagandom," writes August Strindberg, "woman seems almost to have been man's equal. . . . Woman was treated by man with such respect and acted with such self-feeling and freedom, that any such thing in our enlightened times would be considered unheard-of." Ample corroboration of this is found in whatever author one turns to. Mallet affirms: "We find the reverse of all this" (the general condition) "among the Northern nations, who did not so much consider the other sex as made for their pleasure, as to be their equals and companions, whose esteem, as valuable as their other favours, could only be obtained by constant attentions, by generous services, and by a proper exertion of virtue and courage. I conceive that this will at first sight be deemed a paradox, and that it will not be an easy matter to reconcile a manner of thinking which supposes so much delicacy, with the rough, unpolished character of this people. Yet I believe the observation is so well grounded that one may venture to assert that it is this same people who have contributed to diffuse through all Europe that spirit of equity, of moderation and generosity shown by the stronger to the weaker sex, which is at this day the distinguishing characteristic of European manners; nay, that we even owe to them that spirit of gallantry which was so little known to the Greeks and Romans, how polite soever in other respects."

Two things the Norsemen seemed to have understood by instinct—namely, that woman was naturally man's equal, and that the other life was, equally in conformity with nature, a continuation of this, under the same general conditions, aside from a change of physique. Complete sanity, on these two fundamental points, enabled them to lead the sensible life that has never been led since by any nation of Europe, and never will be, until some remedy is found for Christian hallucinations, which see in the other life unspeakable terrors, the most monstrous unrealities, and in the other sex (the true half of the nation as well as the man) a creature little less than an idiot and imbecile. But again it may be asked, how was this "spirit of equity," the political freedom, good laws, and all the other beneficial things in the Norsemen's possession, to be diffused through all Europe, save by the Viking expeditions that have been so much execrated? Were the monkish, or monk-ridden, inhabitants everywhere so docile, so eager for Northern knowledge and enlightenment, that the Norse leaders, splendid orators that they were, could have instilled it all into them through public speaking? Was it their moral duty to go into the land of the enemy as lecturers on reform topics, and to be slaughtered piecemeal by those fiends who knew nothing well but the action of fire on human flesh, or the use of the dagger? Was it possible in those days, and with such a population as the Church had reared, to effect the conquest of thought and republicanism otherwise than through the conquest of the sword? And if this had not been effected, what would the consequences have been to posterity?

But whatever brave leaders and statesmen did, the women of the North were with them, to encourage and stimulate. One gets a new idea of the sex by reading about them. One realizes clearly, by these words of Holmberg's, that no feeble or silly woman could share the thoughts of such men: "We ought above all to draw attention to the fact that there was with these an unquenchable desire for knowledge, a striving for wisdom and a respect for knowledge, which perhaps does not stand forth so plainly in our enlightened time." And this is what he says about their treatment of woman: "With no ancient people has respect for woman been higher, her true value more appreciated, and her rights more extended than with our forefathers. She was, it is true, not the idol, for which one during the age of chivalry kindled incense and brought home the sacrifice of even his human worth—a position which is always unworthy of woman, as founded only on outer charms, and as the step from idol to doll is only a hair's breadth. Still less was she, as with many other races of antiquity, man's passive slave, only existing for his pleasure, or doomed for his comfort to drag forth a joyless and arduous life. The Northern woman's place was right between these two extremes, and such as ought to accrue to her as an important part of the community. She was, as woman always ought to be, *man's equal*, neither more nor less, and this especially when she became a wife. Indeed we do not say too much, if we to woman in pagan times, grant almost the same rights as those she now enjoys, with the only difference that the general respect for her sex was really greater than that paid to it in our time." It must be remembered that these noble words are from the pen of a modern Swede, one of a race who have always accorded woman her due rank. He continues: "Of such respect, such freedom, the Northern woman of antiquity was well deserving for her innate *high-mindedness*. Constantly we find her animated by the same idea as man, by that of freedom, glory, and love of country."

Pigott cites the Sagor for confirmation of the many points of excellence with the Norsemen, this included: "If we consult the Icelandic sagas, many of which are faithful and unpretending pictures of the times in which they were written, we shall find that the Scandinavians were by no means unacquainted with the comforts and even the luxuries of life; that they were skilful mechanics; held music and poetry in the highest esteem; have some claim to the invention of oil-painting, and, above all, in their relations with the weaker sex, showed a degree of refinement and generosity which we may look for in vain amongst the Greeks and Romans in their highest civilization."

There is still another point, not a reform brought about by desperate efforts, through socialism, philanthropy, new financial theories, or the like, but the natural result of wise and good legislation, that has not been mentioned as yet, and that is, the absence of poverty in the North! Mallet speaks of it as a very remarkable feature of Norse government, and indeed it is! He says: "That the leading men of this republic (Iceland) should have framed a code of laws, which, whatever may be their defects, secured at least an ample provision for the poorest members of the community, and suffered no one to perish from starvation, are facts which will always render Iceland peculiarly interesting to all who make human nature—or the development of humanity on earth, in its multifarious and ever-varying aspects—the object of their special attention."

But now we must turn abruptly from this too fascinating contemplation of Norse antiquity, and trace the contrast in religious action, during the Reformation, between the Northern nations and Spain. Bishop Percy, in his preface to Mallet's work, calls attention to *the absence of secrecy* in the religious ceremonies or teachings of the ancient Scandinavians: "But what particularly distinguishes the Celtic institutions from those of the Teutonic nations, is that remarkable air of secrecy and mystery with which the Druids concealed their doctrines from the laity; forbidding that they should ever be committed to writing, and, upon that account, not having so much as an alphabet of their own. In this the institutions of Odin and the Scalds were the very reverse. No barbarous people were so addicted to writing, as appears from the innumerable quantity of Runic inscriptions scattered all over the north; no barbarous people ever held letters in higher reverence, ascribing the invention of them to their chief deity, and attributing to the letters themselves supernatural virtues. Nor is there the least room to believe that any of their doctrines were locked up or concealed from any part of the community. On the contrary, their mythology is for ever displayed in all the songs of their Scalds, just as that of the Greeks and Romans is in the odes of Pindar and Horace. There never existed any institution in which there appears less of reserve and mystery than in that of the Scandinavian people."

It is superfluous to more than allude to the systematic mystery and secrecy of the Christian Church, its Bible, creed, ministration, and all connected with it; I will merely quote what Llorente says about the working of its characteristic institution, the Inquisition: "Secrecy, the foe of truth and justice, was the soul of the tribunal of the Inquisition; it gave to it new life and vigour, sustained and strengthened its arbitrary power, and so emboldened it, that it had the hardihood to arrest the highest and noblest in the land, and enabled it to deceive, by concealing facts, popes, kings, viceroys, and all invested with authority by their sovereign." The "holy office" was in full operation when Columbus went to Spain, and the notorious Torquemada was inquisitor-general; it continued, under imperial support, through several dynasties, but it is our purpose now to consider its work at the time the Reformation was taking firm root in Sweden. The Spaniards would have been less than human if Luther's doctrines had not crept into their minds, too; but the Pope was prepared for this contingency; according to Llorente, "in 1521, the Pope wrote to the governors of the provinces in Castile, during the absence of Charles V., recommending them to prevent the introduction of the works of Luther into the kingdom; and Cardinal Adrian, in the same year, ordered the inquisitors to seize all books of that nature: this order was repeated in 1523." The emperor showed himself no less zealous, for "he commissioned the University of Louvain to form a list of dangerous books, and in 1539 he obtained a bull of approbation from the Pope. The index was published in 1546 by the University in all the states of Flanders, six years after a decree had been issued to prohibit the writings of Luther from being read or bought on pain of death."

In 1529, King Gustaf I. proclaimed Lutheranism the State-religion of Sweden, and soon after deprived the bishops of their name and dignity, prohibited the invoking of saints, the use of holy water, pilgrimages, in short cleared all the Romish mummery out of the kingdom! The Pope and his successors lost their power for ever in the North!

From Spain, however, they extended it to America, under royal protection as usual. "The Spanish possessions in the New World," to quote Arthur Helps, "occupied an immense extent of territory, namely from 40° 43', south latitude, to 37° 48' north latitude, the distances from the Equator, on each side, being nearly the same. Humboldt has observed that the Spanish territory in the New World was not only equal in length to the whole of Africa, but was also of much greater width than the empire of Russia." Accordingly, in this vast dominion Spanish rigour was exercised. The following statements are Llorente's: "Charles V. and Philip II. had regulated the circulation of books in their American states. In 1543 the viceroys and other authorities were commanded to prevent the introduction or printing of tales or romances. In 1550, a new decree obliged the tribunal of the commerce of Seville, to register all the books destined for the colonies, to certify that they were not prohibited. In 1556, the Government commanded that no work relating to the affairs of America should be published without a permission from the Council of the Indies, and that those already printed should not be sold unless they were examined and approved, which obliged all those who possessed any to submit them to the council. The officers of the customs in America were also obliged to seize all the prohibited books which might be imported, and remit them to the archbishops and bishops, who, in this case, possessed the same powers as the inquisitors of Spain. Lastly, Philip II., in 1560, decreed new measures, and the *surveillance* was afterwards as strictly observed in the colonies of the New World as in the peninsula. In the year 1558 the terrible law of Philip II. was published, which decreed the punishments of death and confiscation for all those who should sell, buy, keep, or read the books prohibited by the holy office; and to insure the execution of this sanguinary law, the index was printed, that the people might not allege ignorance in their defence."

Thus, simultaneous with the deliverance of Sweden from the power of Rome and the consequent infliction of the Inquisition there, too, had the ruling monarch shown any weakness or irresolution, this fatal sway was extended over a territory "equal in length to the whole of Africa, and of much greater width than the empire of Russia," in fact, over all that was then known as the New World. Freedom was born again in the North, tyranny forged new fetters in the South!

Yes, Americans, in considering this most frightful of all subjects, must be brought to the harrowing conviction, fraught with the deepest humiliation, that the worst atrocities of the Spanish Inquisition have been perpetrated on American soil, and that *these* were the results of the discovery by Columbus, *these* the scenes enacted in the Spanish colonies! Voltaire has remarked that "an Asiatic, arriving at Madrid on the day of an *auto-da-fé*, would doubt whether it were a festival, religious celebration, sacrifice, or massacre;—it is all of them." The writer of the preface, or advertisement, to Llorente's book, says: "All the records of the fantastic cruelties of the heathen world do not afford so appalling a picture of human weakness and depravity as the authentic and genuine documents of the laws and proceedings of this Holy Office, which professed to act under the influence of the doctrines of the Redeemer of the World!" And the jurisdiction of this Holy Office comprised America!

To revert again to the same authority, Llorente: "In 1570 Philip II. appointed an Inquisition in Mexico, and in 1571 established three tribunals for all America; one at Lima, one in Mexico, and the other at Carthagena, assigning to each the extent of territory which they were to possess, and subjecting them to the authority of the inquisitor-general and the Supreme Council. The first *auto-da-fé*, in Mexico took place in 1574; it was celebrated with so much pomp and splendour, that eye-witnesses have declared that it could only be compared with that of Valladolid in 1559, at which Philip II. and the royal family attended. A Frenchman and an Englishman were burnt as impenitent Lutherans." In Spain there were two *autos-da-fé*, in 1559, against the Lutherans. At the second of these thirteen persons were burnt!

Can doubt any longer remain in the mind of any American, man or woman, as to whether we owe respect and gratitude to Spain, or to the Scandinavian North? Is it not entirely due to the three great Swedish kings, Gustaf Vasa, Carl IX., and Gustaf Adolf, that Spain, "the leader of the Catholic reaction," "the soul and support of the Catholic religion," was frustrated in its intention of bringing the whole world under Catholic dominion? It had made repeated attempts to reestablish Catholicism in Sweden, during the reigns of Johan III., Carl IX., and during the Swedish-Polish war; "it was to restore the Catholic Church that Philip II. desired to obtain the empire of Europe," declares Buckle. This author has very clear ideas about Spain and its religious history, and would educate the world well on this subject, did it but heed; a few brief words of his sum up the record of Philip II.'s work: "Directly that he heard that the Protestants were making converts in Spain, he strained every nerve to stifle the heresy; and so admirably was he seconded by the general temper of the people, that he was able without risk to suppress opinions which convulsed every other part of Europe. In Spain, the Reformation, after a short struggle, died completely away, and in about ten years the last vestige of it disappeared."

BRUÁRÁ RIVER, ON THE ROAD TO THE GEYSER. *Pag. 142.*

CHAPTER VIII.

THE NORSE DISCOVERERS AND COLUMBUS CONTRASTED.

CHRISTOPHER COLUMBUS, " the immortal discoverer of America," as D. Gio. Batista Spotorno calls him, and "that great man to whom we are indebted for the New World," was the true son of his age and his double nationality, Italian-Spanish. His over-mastering desire to discover a new world was not to get away himself from the fetid air of Spain and to secure a refuge, at a safe distance from Spain, for hundreds of thousands of victims of religious persecution, but to gain new territory for the extension of the Gospel and that indispensable appendage of the faith, the Inquisition. We never see in any book treating of him, or that period, that he was shocked at any of the public doings in Spain, or that he was filled with horror at the cruelties that were perpetrated there under his very eyes. A man of a different mould would rather have been burnt at the stake than have been the means of carrying this foul system across the ocean, of running the remotest risk of transplanting it, but Columbus' dearest wish was to become the humble instrument, in the hands of the Lord, of bringing this added glory to the Church and to his sovereigns! Barry, the Roman Catholic author referred to in former chapters of this book, laments that " prejudice, enmity, hostility against the Catholic Church, have the incredible privilege of teaching the Catholic world the life of a man who is one of its most shining glories." Yes, he is safe there, that statement will not be contradicted;

Columbus is indeed one of the most shining glories of the Catholic world; it only remains to be seen how he is estimated outside of this world. "They cannot bring themselves to see" (those prejudiced, hostile biographers he alludes to) "in the discovery of the New World, a providential intervention." No, probably not, with the light that uncorrupted history is now throwing upon the transaction! "They have rejected the superior character of Columbus," he adds, "the man chosen by heaven."

In the prospectus of Prof. Rafn's great work, "Antiquitates Americanæ," there is a declaration to the effect that "it was the knowledge of the Scandinavian voyages, in all probability, which prompted the expedition of Columbus." J. H. Schröeder, a writer in the Swedish periodical *Svea*, believed that news of the Norse discovery had reached Columbus' ears in Italy; Malte-Brun thought the same, and a number of others. Prescott, in his "Ferdinand and Isabella," seems very much puzzled about all this, and says in a foot-note: "It is singular that Columbus, in his visit to Iceland in 1477, should have learned nothing of the Scandinavian voyages to the northern shores of America in the tenth and following centuries; yet, if he was acquainted with them, it appears equally surprising that he should not have adduced the fact in support of his own hypothesis of the existence of land in the west; and that he should have taken a route so different from that of his predecessors in the path of discovery. It may be, however, as M. de Humboldt has well remarked, that the information he obtained in Iceland was too vague to suggest the idea that the lands thus discovered by the Northmen had any connection with the Indies, of which he was in pursuit. In Columbus' day, indeed, so little was understood of the true position of these countries, that Greenland is laid down on the maps in the European seas, and as a peninsular prolongation of Scandinavia."

The author does not take into sufficient consideration the

Roman Catholic talent and propensity for secrecy, especially when the secret is likely to pay well. There were a thousand reasons to one, to prevent this astute southerner from divulging the knowledge he had obtained in Iceland. The princely terms he at last made with their majesties of Spain proves that, whatever other lacks there may have been in his character, there was none of business shrewdness. Besides the blissful certainty he concealed so carefully in his own breast, helped him to bear the long period of waiting. He may have had some objection to the war with Granada on this score, but that it was carried on for the extermination of the Moors did not trouble him. Neither would he have scrupled to take the funds for his equipment on the voyage of discovery, if he had known that they were derived directly from confiscated property, as not unlikely they had been, as they were furnished by Luis de St. Angel, the receiver of the ecclesiastical revenues in Aragon. Columbus had his own ideas of right and wrong, and if Queen Isabella had happened to complain to him, as it is stated she did to others, that "many persons accused her of being influenced in all that she did for the tribunal by a desire to seize the wealth of the condemned," he would have found a way to console her.

Columbus, on the whole, was very fortunately placed; he was not one of those pitiable persons who are in advance of their age; he would have been safe even under the dread eyes of Torquemada; at a period when "there was scarcely a man celebrated for his learning, who had not been prosecuted as a heretic," he was far from likely to reveal a priceless secret for the sake of supporting a scientific hypothesis! No, Columbus was not a scientist in a dangerous sense, else the inquisitor-general would have put a little obstacle in the way of his voyage of discovery. Neither can he be suspected of having read any prohibited Lutheran literature; no heresy crops out in him. He may have beguiled the tedium of his enforced waiting by attending *autos-da-fé*, as any public-spirited citizen naturally would, and he probably saw his share of Lutherans burned, ladies included.

Under all the circumstances, it is a mistake to think that Columbus had any very serious obstacles to contend with, aside from the prevailing stupidity of the age. To be sure, Prescott says that "it cannot be denied that Spain at this period surpassed most of the nations of Christendom in religious enthusiasm, or, to speak more correctly, in bigotry," but Columbus was thoroughly in unison with this spirit, and his experience should not in the slightest degree be confounded with that of thinkers, reformers, scientists, and Lutherans. He had Jesuits and high Church officials for friends and counsellors, one of them Deza himself, the favour and patronage of the Catholic sovereigns, which should be sufficient to save him from ever being classed in that condemned category!

It was a serious inconvenience, certainly, not to have a ship of his own. In the North a gentleman, in those days, had his private vessel, as gentlemen, in our times, have their private carriage, and could go where he liked; but in Spain, the inquisitors, who, in a way, represented the Government, could only seize and confiscate other people's vessels, like the one owned by Burton, an Englishman, whom they burnt as a Lutheran.

The Norse discoverers, on the other hand, were not serious-minded like Columbus, were not burdened with scientific theories, nor a heavy secret, regarded the ocean as little more than a babbling brook, and had more vessels and crews than they knew what to do with. Like our fashionable Americans at the present day, the Norse travellers had been everywhere—almost—and pined for a new coast. So one day they found Greenland, and soon after chanced upon America. They came home and told the news, and then others went. But I will let the Saga relate this, in its own inimitable way: "Bjarni, a very hopeful man. He conceived, when yet young, a desire to travel abroad, and soon earned for himself both riches and respect; and he was every second winter abroad, every other at home with his father. Soon possessed Bjarni his own ship; and the last winter he was in Norway, Herjulf prepared for a voyage to Greenland with Eric. . . . Bjarni came to Eyrar with his ship the summer of the same year in which his father had sailed away in spring. These tidings appeared serious to Bjarni, and he was unwilling to unload his ship. Then his seamen asked him what he would do; he answered that he intended to continue his custom, and pass the winter with his father." In all this we see the cultivated, travelled gentleman, fond also of home-life and home-ties. In the rest of his reply, however, he quite transcends any gentleman, or any mariner, we have heard of: "'And I will,' said he, 'bear for Greenland, if ye will give me your company.'" The crew proved quite as remarkable as he, it seemed to be a holiday-trip for the whole of them; far from demurring, they answered, that "they would follow his counsel." Then said Bjarni: "'Imprudent will appear our voyage, since no one of us has been in the Greenland ocean.' However, they put to sea as soon as they were ready."

And this was all there was to it. Money, men, vessel, provisions, everything needful they had; the only thing they did not have was knowledge of the route, but that was not serious. They made about as quick a voyage as if they had known the way, and besides their destination (which had been discovered before) it is thought that the lands discovered by Bjarni Herjulfson on that impromptu trip, gathered from the details and minute description of the voyages, were Connecticut, Long Island, Rhode Island, Massachusetts, Nova Scotia, and Newfoundland.

When poor Columbus, provided with royal promises and patronage, large funds, and all that his southern heart could wish, returned to Palos, to make immediate preparations for his voyage, he found that his difficulties had just begun.

Washington Irving did not mean the description of this to be ludicrous, and perhaps it would not be to one who had not read of Bjarni's start-off beforehand: "The inhabitants considered the ships and crews demanded of them in the light of sacrifices devoted to destruction. The owners of vessels refused to furnish them for so desperate a service, and the boldest seamen shrunk from such a wild and chimerical cruise into the wilderness of the ocean. ... Nothing can be a stronger evidence of the bold nature of this undertaking, than the extreme dread with which it was regarded by a maritime community, composed of some of the most adventurous navigators of the age."

This was in 1492, and the Norse party sailed on their little pleasure-trip in 982. Does it not seem as if retrogression, and not progress, marked the stages of history? As if the Darwinian theory was sadly true—*in a reverse sense*, from man to ape? The Norse voyagers started off merrily, anticipating enjoyment; the Spaniards in a state of abject terror; they evidently stood in greater dread of a long voyage than of the Inquisition, but, to be sure, fire was their favourite element. By going on the ocean, also, they were leaving all the peaceful and congenial scenes of their native land. When at last, after months of delay, they set sail from Palos, a lot of sorry, whimpering mourners, they confessed themselves to Juan Perez, as a matter of course, partook of the communion, and went through a lot of devout and affecting ceremonials, committing themselves to the especial guidance and protection of Heaven. It is well known that the men behaved as badly as an undisciplined and mutinous crew could behave, all the way over; and when at last one of the seamen saw land,—not the grand seignor, Christopher Columbus, who was not born to be in the advance-guard,—the incipient admiral coolly swooped off the promised reward, and let the poor sailor die of despair.

They landed with great pomp, as could be supposed. They did everything with pomp those Spaniards, performed all their ante-mortem cremations with pomp, slaughtered with pomp, and confiscated and robbed with pomp, in fact, kept up such a blaze that the heavenly kingdom could never have been quite free from the smoke so continually ascending. Smoke was the daily bulletin of their political and religious operations. Columbus clad himself as behoved his mixed character of admiral, viceroy, devotee, priest, *pro tem.*, discoverer, and crusader; scarlet, the fire-colour, being conspicuous amid his armour; and bearing aloft those symbols that would make manifest his allegiance to the twin powers of evil, Church and Throne, "his first act, after prayers and thanksgiving, was to call upon all present to take the oath of obedience to him as admiral and viceroy, representing the persons of the sovereigns."

If the Norsemen had done anything of this kind they would certainly have thought that they had taken leave of their senses. This was the superior civilization, the Christian civilization, attained by Spain five hundred years afterwards!

Bjarni went back to Norway, evidently making the return trip with as little difficulty as the one to the new shores, and told Erik Jarl about his voyages—the Jarl receiving him well—and that he had seen unknown lands. But to resume the racy narrative from the "Codex Flatoiensis": "People thought that he had shown no curiosity, when he had nothing to relate about those countries, and this became somewhat of a matter of reproach to him. . . . There was now much talk about voyages of discovery. Leif, the son of Eric the Red, of Brattahlid, went to Bjarni Herjulfson and bought the ship of him, and engaged men for it, so that there were thirty-five men in all."

He went to Bjarni Herjulfson and bought the ship of him and engaged men for it! But Columbus—Was that Norseman, Leif, in the year 984 or 985, in such a savage state as not to know that the way to proceed in such a vast undertaking as that of crossing the ocean to unknown lands, was to present a petition at court, seeking first the mediation of some high dignitary of the Church,—he could have found a stray bishop or two, if he had tried, among the early converts,—to make extortionate demands for himself, in the way of money, commissions, and perquisites, and appointments, after having thrown Bjarni overboard in the first place? But this arrogant and lawless barbarian had money enough of his own, bought a ship off hand, with less concern than a Spaniard, five hundred years afterwards, would have bought a plaster image of a saint, did not even make known his intentions to the ruling sovereign nor consult a priest, but was in all things quite sufficient unto himself. To continue the narrative: "Now prepared they their ship, and sailed out into the sea when they were ready"—without confessing themselves, or partaking of the communion, or going through devout and affecting ceremonials, or committing themselves to the especial guidance and protection of Heaven, the godless pagans!—"and then found that land first which Bjarni had found last." They went ashore and explored. After that they sailed out to sea and found another land, and went ashore there, too, touching in turn Newfoundland, Labrador, and Nantucket. Then they shaped their course through Nantucket Bay, beyond the south-western extremity of Cape Cod; thence across the mouth of Buzzard's Bay to Seaconnet Passage, and up the Pocasset River to Mount Hope Bay. "After this took they counsel, and formed the resolution of remaining there for the winter, and built three large houses. . . . But when they had done with the house-building, Leif said to his comrades"—(*comrades?* Columbus had no comrades; *he* took the oath of allegiance from a servile crew!)—"'Now will I divide our men into two parts and have the land explored.' . . . Leif was a great and strong man, grave and well-favoured, therewith sensible and moderate in all things. . . . And Leif gave the land a name after its qualities and called it *Vinland*." (Hence also the modern name of Martha's Vineyard.)

As one of their experiences, they happened to come to some men on a rock out at sea; as it turned out they were the shipwrecked Icelanders, Thorer and his wife Gudrid, who had been in quest of the same new shores. Not knowing who they were, however, Leif showed his customary good sense and kindness of heart. "'Now let us,' said Leif, 'hold our wind, so that we come up to them, if they should want our assistance, and the necessity demands that we should help them; and if they should not be kindly disposed, the power is in our hands and not in theirs.'"

How different would have been the Spanish mode of procedure had one of Columbus' vessels stumbled upon a lot of strange men on a rock! We can see, in imagination, the frantic ejaculations, hear the pious cry, "Holy Virgin, protect us!" and gathering courage from seeing the defenceless condition of the poor ship-wrecked wretches, the Spaniards would probably have rushed upon them and massacred them in a body, and found out afterwards that they were countrymen of theirs! However, a few deaths, more or less, do not count.

"Now there was much talk about Leif's voyage to Vinland, and Thorvald, his brother, thought that the land had been much too little explored. Then said Leif to Thorvald: 'Thou canst go with my ship, brother! if thou wilt, to Vinland.' . . . Now Thorvald made ready for this voyage, with thirty men, and took counsel thereon with Leif, his brother. Then made they their ship ready and put to sea, and nothing is told of their voyage until they came to Leif's booths in Vinland. There they laid up their ship and spent a pleasant winter, and caught fish for their support."

In the summer they explored the land, the western part of it, and the following summer they went eastward. Comparing Columbus with the Norse voyagers, Aaron Goodrich cites an incident in Thorvald's experience, to illustrate the different characteristics of the two: "Attacked by hostile Indians, Thorvald says: 'We shall defend ourselves as well as we can, but not use our weapons much against them.' Greeted by peaceable Indians, Columbus orders the ship's gun fired in the midst, in order 'to abate their pride and make them not contemn the Christians.'" He says also, as the narrative has already told us, that "all the Norse leaders, Bjarne Herjulfson, Leif and Thorvald Ericson, Karlsefne, Bjarne Grimolfson, worked for the common good, and were as much loved and respected by their followers as Columbus was hated and despised by his."

Goodrich also draws a just comparison in regard to the extent of exploration of each party, and says: "If the discovery by Columbus in 1492 of the islands of San Salvador and San Domingo was the discovery of the continent of America, then the discovery and permanent colonization of Iceland and Greenland, six hundred years before by the Scandinavians, was also the discovery of that continent; the portion of mainland coasted by Columbus was avowedly but small, and he professed to be in Asia. The Northmen, on the contrary, visited all the eastern coast of America, from the extreme north to Florida, formed settlements, and for centuries carried on commerce with the products of what are now the most civilized, populous and enlightened portions of America; and the American might well feel relief and pride at the knowledge that the first of his race to touch upon his native shores were the heroic Norsemen—

> 'Kings of the main, their leaders brave,
> Their barks the dragons of the wave.'"

Toulmin Smith, in his "Discovery of America by the Northmen," argues each point, and seems to have chosen the dialogue form for his book in order to debate every inch of ground with the defenders of Columbus. He dissects Bancroft's entire statement relative to both in the most scathing way. His summing up is this: "Columbus was *not* the discoverer of America; he was *not* the first visitant to her shores; his act was *not* so perilous, or complete, or adventurous a one as the oft-repeated acts of the Northmen; nor was his actual knowledge of the country in any degree so exact, while all his ideas concerning it were purely erroneous. . . . Shall the Northmen be deprived, then, of the well-deserved meed of honour and glory which is so justly due to them, for their bold and enterprising achievements, for their often-repeated explorations, and for their early but accurate knowledge of these distant regions?"

Happy for Columbus if he could be let off with a comparison with the discoverers and colonists, Bjarni, Leif, and Thorvald, but there is still another distinguished Norseman, whose biography and character belittle the inglorious Italian fortune-hunter still more, and this man is Thorfinn Karlsefne. Illustrious, influential, possessing immense wealth and a lineage so splendid as only to be equalled by his celebrated line of descendants, Karlsefne was a truly remarkable man, and him must the American people honour as their first worthy colonist. "Snorre, his son, was born in Vinland, A.D. 1007. From him, according to a genealogical table" (affirms E. F. Slafter) "introduced into 'Antiquitates Americanæ' by Prof. Rafn, are lineally descended a large number of distinguished Scandinavians. Among them we note the following: Snorre Sturleson, the celebrated historian, born 1178; Bertel Thorvaldson, the eminent sculptor, born 1770; Finn Magnusen, born 1781; Birgin Thorlacius, professor in Copenhagen, born 1775; Grim Thorkelin, professor in Copenhagen and many others earlier in the line." In a note, in this edition of the Norse voyages, published by the Prince Society, it is stated that "it would appear that Karlsefne himself narrated originally the events that occurred on these voyages, and that only the more important portions were written out by the sagaman; that it was not written till a numerous race of distinguished men had descended from Karlsefne."

"Thorfinn took to trading voyages," says the narrative, "and was thought an able seaman and merchant. . . . One summer

Karlsefne fitted out his ship, and purposed a voyage to Vinland." And now follows an example of the lavish hospitality of the Norsemen, showing the grand scale upon which they exercised it: " Leif, on his side, showed them hospitality, and bade the crews of these two ships home, for the winter, to his own house at Brattahlid. This the merchants accepted and thanked him. Then were their goods removed to Brattahlid; there was no want of large out-houses to keep the goods in, neither plenty of everything that was required, wherefore they were well satisfied in the winter. But towards Yule"—the Norse *jul* which the Church appropriated and converted into the Christian Christmas, a season of extreme festivity in the North, devoid of tedious religious ceremonies—" Leif began to be silent, and was less cheerful than he used to be. One time Karlsefne turned towards Leif and said : ' Hast thou any sorrow, Leif, my friend? People think to see that thou art less cheerful than thou wert wont to be; thou hast entertained us with the greatest splendour, and we are bound to return it to thee with such services as we can command ; say now, what troubles thee?' Leif answered : ' Ye are friendly and thankful, and I have no fear as concerns our intercourse, that ye will feel the want of attention ; but, on the other hand, I fear that when ye come elsewhere it will be said that ye have never passed a worse Yule than that which now approaches.' " With the aid of the resources on Thorfinn's two vessels, freely offered for his host's use, the joyful holidays could be duly kept, and Thorer having died, some time since, the occasion was rendered yet more festive by the wedding of Thorfinn and Gudrid, Thorer's widow.

And notwithstanding the extensive explorations that had been made, " in Brattahlid," says the narrative, " began people to talk much about, that Vinland the Good should be explored."

Columbus could not give up his time to exploration, in the strict sense of the word, for he was engaged in gold-hunting and pondering how to turn his discovery to speedy account. The

Norsemen, as Goodrich clearly demonstrates, "were actuated by motives far different from those of Columbus; they did not come in search of gold or slaves, but to gather by industry the natural products of the land, carrying on therewith a flourishing trade between the continent, Greenland, Iceland, and Norway." He adds his testimony also to the fact of the prevailing ignorance in Europe, by stating that "letters and learning flourished in Iceland when the rest of Europe was intellectually stagnant; histories and annals are therefore copious."

The Norsemen manifestly had a gift for navigating, exploring, and colonizing, while Columbus, better fitted for an ecclesiastical calling or for a crusader, and with mind distraught by visions of the holy sepulchre, which he was some time to recover, after he had found his gold-mine, proceeded laboriously and with infinite difficulty. What made the Norsemen such skilful and daring navigators it is superfluous to state, but as Laing very wittily observes: "Ferocity, ignorance, and courage will not bring men across the ocean." History does not relate to us for our malicious gratification what were Columbus' reflections, in Iceland, when reading of these Norse voyages, or rather he did not commit his bitter and envious thoughts to writing, but the anecdote Laing repeats about Charlemagne will serve very well to indicate what he must have felt at the bare mention of their bold doings, no doubt recounted to him with Icelandic enthusiasm and national pride. This is the story of the French proselyter: "Historians te us that when Charlemagne, in the ninth century, saw some piratical vessels of the Northmen cruising at a distance in the Mediterranean, to which they had for the first time found their way, that he turned away from the window and burst into tears. Was it the barbarism of these pirates, or their civilization, their comparative superiority in the art of navigation, and of all belonging to it that moved him? None of the countries under his sway, none of the Christian populations of Europe in the seventh, eighth, or ninth centuries, had ships and men capable of such a voyage. The comparative state of shipbuilding and navigation, in two countries with sea-coasts, is a better test of their comparative civilization and advance in all the useful arts than that of their church-building."

But this was the superiority of contemporaries! What if Charlemagne with his over-sensitive self-love, had been transferred to Columbus' age and been compelled to acknowledge, if even in his secret soul, the superior civilization, and the superiority in the art of navigation of a race of ferocious, barbarous, Christian-hating pagans, who had lived half a millenary before? This would have been the refinement of suffering to Columbus, if he had been intelligent enough to perceive it; but he was not. A wise man, with some little knowledge of his own incapacity, would have forsworn navigation, after studying those documents in Iceland; but Columbus persisted, missed the route and still persisted, and knew nothing of geography till the day of his death.

It must also have annoyed Charlemagne excessively to know that democracy was carried to such an extent in the North, that every ambitious leader could have his own vessel! Laing calls attention to this, with the rest: "It is to be observed also that the ships of the Northmen in those ages did not belong to the king, or to the State, but to private adventurers and peasants, and were fitted out by them." If Columbus had read in the *Saga* that "Bjarni possessed his own ship," and that Leif, when he made up his mind to start on a voyage of discovery, "bought the ship of him and engaged men for it," without any pother or delay, the recollection of these two little facts could not have sweetened his own fourteen years of waiting for funds, vessels, and royal patronage.

It is no exaggeration for Wheaton to say of the men of the North: "Their familiarity with the perils of the ocean, and with the diversified manners and customs of foreign lands, stamped their national character with bold and original features, which distinguished them from every other people." But little did these men dream, with all their proud ambition, that the classic antiquity they created in the North would yet stand forth, *one thousand years afterwards*, as the scene of extinct virtues and traits, of acts so bold and original, that no subsequent race has ever attempted to repeat them, and that have always been regarded as little short of fabulous!

Still, Columbus made a sufficiently good use of his time and opportunities to be able to return to Spain in the guise of a great discoverer and magnate, and in Las Casas' description of his reception at Barcelona, we are told that "a modest smile lighted up his features, showing that he enjoyed the state and glory in which he came." His situation, for all that, was precarious; he had excited rather too much sordid expectation in a court and a land whose insatiate cry was ever gold, souls! gold, souls! So one day, after his return to the New World, he wrote a letter to their majesties in Spain, from which a paragraph has already been quoted in this book; even Irving disapproves of this letter and the suggestions it contains, and comments thus: "Among the many sound and salutary suggestions in this letter, there is one of a most pernicious tendency, written in that mistaken view of natural rights prevalent at the day, but fruitful of so much wrong and misery in the world. Considering that the greater the number of these cannibal pagans transferred to the Catholic soil of Spain, the greater would be the number of souls put in the way of salvation, he proposed to establish an exchange of them as slaves, against live stock, to be furnished by merchants to the colony. The ships to bring such stock were to be landed nowhere but at the island of Isabella, where the Carib captives would be ready for delivery. A duty was to be levied on each slave for the benefit of the royal revenue. In this way the colony would be furnished with all kinds of live stock free of expense; the peaceful islands would be freed from warlike and inhuman neighbours; the

M

royal treasury would be greatly enriched, and a vast number of souls would be snatched from perdition, and carried, as it were, by main force to heaven."

So much for the suggestion, the details of the plan; but it did not stop at that; Irving goes on to say: "In his eagerness to produce immediate profit, and to indemnify the sovereigns for those expenses which bore hard upon the royal treasury, he sent, likewise, about five hundred Indian prisoners, who, he suggested, might be sold as slaves at Seville. It is painful to find the brilliant renown of Columbus sullied by so foul a stain, and the glory of his enterprises degraded by such flagrant violations of humanity."

If Irving had taken the pains to read the narratives of the Norse voyages, and to ascertain the merits of the case, he would have turned his sympathies into a nobler channel, and spared himself the pain of being shocked at anything that Columbus said or did. With such a key to the character of the man as that yielded by the Iceland episode, in 1477, this based upon Columbus' anticipation of what he would obtain at Iceland, Irving would have realized that nothing could sully a character so uniformly bad and unprincipled as the one he made the subject of his biography. His wicked work was continued, for in 1496 Don Bartholomew Columbus sent three hundred slaves to Spain, from Hispaniola; in course of time Indian slavery was varied with African, and "in 1552," as stated in Arthur Helps' "Spanish Conquest in America," "Philip the Second concluded a bargain for the grant of a monopoly to import 23,000 negroes into the Indies; and so this traffic went on until the great *assiento* of 1713, between the English and the Spanish Governments was concluded, respecting the importation of negroes into Spanish America. The number of negroes imported into America from the year 1517, when the trade was first permitted by Charles V., to 1807, the year in which the British Parliament passed the act abolishing the slave-trade, cannot be estimated at less than five or six millions."

The present age, as little as the past, owes gratitude to Columbus; praise is not due to him for anything that he did, while the blame is too heavy to be dealt adequately. Better than to waste valuable time in contemplating this deeply culpable and bigoted man, would be to consign both him and the miserable country that fostered his dishonest purposes, to a swift forgetfulness. We have that with which we can profitably occupy our thoughts: the deeds of our own indomitable ancestors!

Daniel Wilson, in his "Prehistoric Man," before adding the weight of his testimony also to the truth of the Norse discovery of America, aptly cites these words of the great Niebuhr: "He who calls what has vanished back into being enjoys a bliss like that of creating." This is the glad duty of the American Republic, to call the grand Scandinavian antiquity back into being, and to continue the progress started so nobly in the pagan North, as if there had been no intermission, caused by the "antinaturalists" of Southern Europe, for one thousand years! Let us continue where they left off; we shall not find much of value in the intervening ages; we shall only see Spain's foul autograph scrawled on every fair nation in Europe, except the Northern ones, and on half the American continent!

The paragraph of Daniel Wilson's referred to is this: "From the appearance of the 'Antiquitates Americanæ,' accordingly, may be dated the systematic resolve of American antiquaries and historians to find evidence of intercourse with the ancient world prior to that recent year of the fifteenth century in which the ocean revealed its great secret to Columbus. From the literary memorials of the Norsemen, thus brought to light, we glean sufficient evidence to place beyond doubt not only the discovery and colonization of Greenland, by Eric the Red—apparently in the year 985—but also the exploration of more southern lands, some of which, we can scarcely doubt, must have formed part of the American continent. Of the authenticity of the manuscripts from whence these narratives are derived there is not the slightest room for question."

This chapter would not be complete without the words of Hubert Howe Bancroft on this all-important question: "Mr. B. F. de Costa, in a carefully studied monograph on the subject, assures us that there can be no doubt as to their authenticity, and I am strongly inclined to agree with him. It is true that no less eminent authors than George Bancroft and Washington Irving have expressed opinions in opposition to De Costa's views, but it must be remembered that neither of these distinguished gentlemen made a very profound study of the Icelandic Sagas, indeed Irving directly states that he 'has not had the means of tracing this story to its original sources ;' nor must we forget that neither the author of the 'Life of Columbus,' nor he of the 'History of the Colonization of the United States,' could be expected to willingly strip the laurels from the brow of his familiar hero, Christopher Columbus, and concede the honour of the 'first discovery' to the Northern sea-kings, whose exploits are so vaguely recorded."

It is the office of the American people, as a nation, to strip these laurels from the brow of a man made great by a glory he stole!

CHURCH AND PARLIAMENT HOUSE, REYKJAVIK.

Page 165.

CHAPTER IX.

THE BENEFICIAL RESULTS TO THE PRESENT AGE AND POSTERITY OF ATTRIBUTING THIS MOMENTOUS DISCOVERY TO THE TRUE PERSONS.

HAD the vast literature of Iceland preserved in the retentive and faithful memories of its scalds and sagamen, the annals of what was in many respects an ideal civilization, describing the life of a race mentally and physically sound, whose thoughts, words and acts were strong and vigorous—had this literature existed in a written or printed form, in any tangible form, at the introduction of Christianity in the North, it would undoubtedly have shared the fate of the pagan literature of other countries. The destruction of immense quantities of the works of Grecian and Roman anti-Christian writers signalized the imposition of this faith in the Roman empire, and the destruction of temples and images, of all relics of the Odin and Thor worship in Scandinavia, is a sufficient indication of the fate that would have befallen books and manuscripts, had there been any for the priests and bishops to lay hands on. But, to the supreme good fortune of future generations, this was preserved where the Christian desecrators could not enter, it was safely guarded behind spiritual bolts and bars, in the faithful and reverent minds of the people, and long after, not much before the seventeenth century, when the nations of Europe, after the first decisive revolt represented in the Reformation, had begun to recover from the asphyxia into which the unnatural and preposterous doctrines of the Christian religion had thrown them, Icelandic history was made known to them, the revelation of a system of ethics, of a moral code, of political and social regulations and customs so unlike those which Christian Europe had adopted and lived after, that it could not at first produce anything but astonishment and very partial understanding. Had any one realized then that this history of an enlightened past threatened the existence of the unenlightened condition in which the modern world was sunk, there would have been an effort made to suppress these writings as soon as they appeared. As it was, the public, and the guardians of the public weal, were too enervated to realize the moral force contained in the Sagas, and too secure in the belief that the Christian religion would endure for all time, and was really impervious to assault, to take any precautions.

Although the reader has again and again been asked to consider the great value and importance of this ancient literature, there are still some opinions in regard to it that must not be overlooked. Beamish, referring to Iceland, has said: "There the unerring memories of the scalds and sagamen were the depositories of past events, which, handed down from age to age, in one unbroken line of historical tradition, were committed to writing on the introduction of Christianity (A.D. 1000), and now come before us with an internal evidence of their truth which places them among the highest order of historic records." In an address before the Historical Society of Rhode Island on the visits of the Northmen to that state, Alexander Farnum uttered words that will have much weight with Americans: "At first sight it seems a remarkable circumstance that nine centuries ago, when the literature of continental Europe presents so little of value or interest, we should find on the remote, inhospitable shores of Iceland a body of men who carefully studied the past and closely observed the present, and whose recollections when committed to record on the introduction of

Christianity and the art of writing became at once an historical literature such as hardly any contemporary nation of Europe could rival." William Cullen Bryant says: "These sagas were reduced to writing by diligent and studious men; inestimable treasures laid up for the use of future historians."

But the noblest tribute of all is that from Professor W. Fiske, called by Samuel Kneeland "the most learned cultivator of these Northern languages in this country:" "It (the old Icelandic literature) deserves the careful study of every student of letters. For the English-speaking races, especially, there is nowhere, so near home, a field promising to the scholar so rich a harvest. The few translations, or attempted translations, which are to be found in English, give merely a faint idea of the treasures of antique wisdom and sublime poetry which exist in the Eddic lays, or of the quaint simplicity, dramatic action, and striking realism which characterize the historical sagas." To strengthen the testimony still more, I cite B. F. De Costa: "Yet while other nations were without a literature, the intellect of Iceland was in active exercise, and works were produced like the Eddas and Heimskringla, works, which, being inspired by a lofty genius, will rank with the writings of Homer and Herodotus." The Howitts even assert that "the Icelandic poems have no parallel in all the treasures of ancient literature; they are the expressions of the souls of poets existing in the primeval and uneffeminated earth. The Edda is a structure of that grandeur and importance, that it deserves to be far better known to us than it is. The spirit in it is sublime and colossal."

In the sentence, "*they are the expressions of the souls of poets existing in the primeval and uneffeminated earth*," the pith of the whole matter is reached. The sagas, whether poetical or prose, do indeed relate of a life diametrically opposite from that of which we are now cognisant; of an earth which some cause has essentially changed. These poets, and all who formed the chief characters in the Northern epics, had a different ideal from that of the rest of Europe; their standard was not the idealization of suffering, but the conquest of suffering, that is, of all the weakness, sickliness, depravity, moral feebleness and evil of all kinds that produce it; all this the pagans of the North crushed out as pertinaciously as it was engendered by the Christian communities in which suffering was the only ideal. The Norsemen believed that human nature was good, capable of whatever the individual in his highest pride might will; the Romanists believed that human nature was evil, and that the will was the worst snare; to one class the earth was a perfectly satisfactory field of activity, which could be rendered all that man could wish, to the other a den of misery, hopeless from the beginning.

The value of this literature, this history of the North, which from all accounts seems to be the only reliable history we have, is that it describes, with that graphic force yielded by truth alone, a state of society founded on natural principles. At this late hour the people of the nineteenth century are beginning to yield some slight reverence to nature, and depute science to tell them what nature is. What little has been learned regarding the physical laws has scarcely extended as yet to the domain of moral and spiritual laws; an entrance has been forced to the one, but the Church, as of old, forbids access to the other. The race moulded and fashioned by the Bible, who are aching in every limb from the cramp it has caused, have the inestimable privilege of reading of a race who had no Bible to warp them out of all human shape, and who were as they were created to be. The conclusion is unavoidable that the people of the North were so totally unlike any other nation because they were wholly untinctured with Christianity; thence their strength of character, their intrepidity, their marked individuality, the large results consequent upon their every act. Mr. Bryant remarks, half humorously: "The Northmen had a genius for discovering new countries by accident," and they really did accomplish more, even in other directions, by mere chance, than others accomplished by the most painful efforts, proving Emerson's words that "it is as easy for the strong man to be strong, as for the weak to be weak." The nature that they had never defied or insulted was their constant ally.

But the two elements could not live conjoined in Europe; one or the other had to go under. Christianity, the prostitution of nature, won the victory over the natural life, and the North, too, finally accepted the teachings that pronounce man vile. From that hour the darkness settled swiftly over all Europe and the Middle Ages chronicled the complete sway of the Church. The Scandinavian nations had at last been redeemed from barbarism. To this triumph of the Church we are told that we are to ascribe the blessings of modern civilization; indeed this is the prevailing theory. It is this crazy theory which the Icelandic history, treasured up for this present age, is to dispel, its province being to rectify an error in which the European race have lived for eighteen hundred years and to which they still stubbornly cling. The extinction of Northern paganism, so-called, but more properly of Northern irreligion, ought to have demonstrated clearly that under the shadow of Christianity nothing else could live; it affiliates with nothing else, and never can.

Felix Oswald shows very forcibly this lack of homogeneity between Christianity and that which is alleged to be inseparable from it: "But in examining the claims of these theorists," he says, "the impartial inquirer cannot overlook the following objections: 1. That the rise of the Christian faith coincides with the sunset of the great South-European civilization; 2. That the zenith of its power coincides with the midnight of mediæval barbarism; 3. That the decline of its influence coincides with the sunrise of a North-European civilization; 4. That all the principal victories of Freedom and Science have been achieved in spite of the Church, in spite of her utmost efforts to thwart or diminish their triumph, that only in consequence of the futility of these efforts the heresies of one age have become the truisms of the next, so that Christianity has always marched in the rear of civilization ; 5. That the exponents of the Christian dogmas persist in their hostility to the progress of a reform which they recognize only by condescending to share the fruits of its former victories ; 6. That the worst enemies of political and intellectual liberty were firm believers in the dogmas of the New Testament, while the direct or indirect repudiation of those dogmas has been the fundamental tenet of nearly every great thinker, scholar or statesmen, till the degree of *Protestantism* has become the chief test of intellectual sanity ; 7. That among the contemporary nations of the Christian world, the most sceptical are the most civilized, while the most orthodox are the most backward in freedom, industry and general intelligence."

These are objections which Christian believers do not attempt to explain away ; their only strength lies in ignoring facts and in maintaining their assertions in the face of truth. If we look back across the black chasm of the Middle Ages, we see an uncontaminated soil, up there in the North, on which were no prisons, brothels, houses of correction, churches, charitable institutions or court-houses; and in Iceland, where the brightness concentrated, a state of society in which freedom, happiness and prosperity were not postponed till the millennium. How was it possible for Iceland to preserve the proudest national position on record for four hundred years, to become the model of a republic, and almost the sole intellectual repository in Europe ? How was it possible for this remote and desolate island to conserve so much moral force, so much of the essence of its own transcendent power and genius, as to revive the flagging energies of the modern world and reveal to it the long road of its stupid and imbecile retrogression, every step of which must be retraced, until the stragglers get back to first principles? And why cannot the American Republic, with its brilliant opportunities, reach the same moral and intellectual height that the Republic of Iceland attained one thousand years ago? The fault does not lie with Americans, with their Government or their Constitution, but in the insidious evil wrought by the Christian emissaries in their midst. If they had made the whole structure of society secular, as well as their Constitution, reduced Sunday to the level of other days, the Bible to the level of other books, churches and cathedrals to the level of other buildings, unconsecrated, and allowed to be used only for useful purposes, priests and clergymen to the level of other men, nay, below that, to the level of idlers and beneficiaries, who, pursuing no useful calling, live on the community and impoverish it, the nation would have made enormous progress, and history could again have recorded the almost fabulous deeds of indomitable and grandly ambitious men! As it is, all the vices and abominations of Europe have been transplanted there; in American cities are to be seen the pomp and mummery of cathedral service, the squalor of the worst poverty, the brazen infamy of the lowest crime and depravity, just as in Europe. Is it because the Constitution of the United States has germinated the same evils as Russian, or Spanish, or German, or English monarchy? Is it because "human nature is the same, all over the world," as those who despise it are fond of saying? Or is it because the Church germinates the same evils everywhere, under a republic or under a monarchy, because the Church produces a certain species of human nature, which chokes out all others, and thus gives a certain show of truth to the trite saying that human nature is the same, all over the world, for the people of the United States have given the Christian idolaters full freedom to carry on their work. The Christian nature is undoubtedly the same all over the world: hypocritical, canting, secretive, avaricious, deeply designing and Machiavellian; each leader makes a tool and dupe of his followers; congregations do their priest's or minister's bidding, and the whole society is permeated with their spirit and purpose. We do not know what *human* nature is; we have not seen it; we have only seen the regeneration effected by the Church. We can *read* about it, however, in the old Norse sagas, and in some blessed hour this will rouse the desire in all who read to become human and natural again, to shake off this palsying superstition that has benumbed heart and mind for so many ages. Listening to the twaddle of the priests and Bible interpreters, we had almost forgotten that we possessed any capabilities akin to those of the Icelandic republicans of the olden time.

When will it become possible for Americans to do away with church-taxation, with religious holidays and fasts, with penal servitude, with poverty, with prostitution, with unhappy marriages, with the life-long misery of nine-tenths of those born to the earth? Hospitality, but one of the many virtues of the Norsemen, in and of itself did much to prevent poverty and at all events prevented any one from dying of starvation. But hospitality, in the broad sense understood by the Norsemen, is despised by their English and American descendants, in fact by all civilized nations. In speaking of the hospitality everywhere shown by the natives of the islands he visited to Columbus, Irving observes: "The untutored savage, in almost every part of the world, scorns to make a traffic of hospitality." This traffic, together with the slave-traffic, the woman-traffic, the soul-traffic, was introduced by Christianity; everything must be bought and paid for, from bread to absolution. Human beings had no rights; whatever blessings they enjoyed were by grace; food and shelter were costly luxuries, to be earned, never to be given. If a little hungry boy steals a loaf of bread, Christian England sends him to gaol and condemns him to a month of hard labour. Famishing adults, in Europe or America, can only get food on credit if their promise to pay is good. In Iceland, even at the present day, there is said to be only one prison, a good, strong one, but with no one in it. There are no inns, and hospitality is the custom. But the other nations allow the Icelanders to starve, in case of famine.

Samuel Kneeland, in his exceedingly interesting book, "An American in Iceland," describing the visit of a party of Americans to this famous island at the time of the Millennial celebration, says that there is a remarkable revival of the old Icelandic literary spirit in the present century, as exhibited by their poets, historians, linguists and journalists. "The present mental cultivation of the people," he affirms, "is very high. . . . The common people are well acquainted with their own and other national histories, ancient and modern; they know all about the early discovery of America by the Northmen, five centuries before Columbus, while very few of us, until recently, knew any more of Iceland than we did of the South Pole, or the wilds of Africa."

After bestowing many encomiums upon these proud, independent people, who he declares are "born republicans," he says: "And now I trust that the reader will admit that Iceland was justified in proclaiming to the nations the celebration of her one thousandth anniversary; that she deserves the admiration of the civilized world for what she has done for liberty, the advance of knowledge, and the preservation of historic records, at a time when the rest of Europe was in darkness; and especially that she has proved that man is superior to his surroundings, and that hardship, oppression and poverty can neither stifle the aspirations for liberty, nor degrade a poetic and heroic race."

"Hardship, oppression and poverty" have been the more modern experience of Iceland, coming with the Christian dispensation. It was not poor emigrants that first sought her shores, nor those belonging to the common people. A bleak and sterile land could never induce what Christianity and subjection to the throne of Norway induced almost immediately. In Pigott's mention of this fact that in 1262 Iceland was united to the crown of Norway, the pregnant sentence follows, already quoted : " But all interest in public affairs thenceforth died away, and no Sagas were written, because there was nothing to write about." This was the case all over Europe ; there was really nothing to write about until the " revival of letters " in the seventeenth century. " In Europe generally," as Buckle states, " the seventeenth century was distinguished by the rise of a secular literature in which ecclesiastical theories were disregarded." By a ludicrous coincidence, remarked upon by several Swedish authors, St. Birgitta was the first person to make Sweden known, in modern times, and Gustaf Vasa, the second. The worthy woman mercifully freed Sweden from her presence and went to Rome, to seek a broader field of activity; while Gustaf Vasa obliterated her work, in Vadstena, and in Sweden generally, and cleared the land thenceforth of all saints. But previous to this, all three of the Scandinavian nations, as well as Iceland, had sunk into a decline ; there had been five hundred years of Roman delirium ; pageants, pilgrimages, baptismal rites, miracles, saint-worship, throughout the North, but in a somewhat modified form : religious zeal and fanaticism could never run quite to the same excess there as in Southern Europe, but yet Gustaf Vasa rose in opposition none too soon. As it was, silly, superstitious legends superseded the Sagas, and slinking, black-gowned monks trod Norse soil. The splendid realities which only began to pale toward the year 1000, had become fabulous things of the past, bearing so little resemblance to existing conditions, that they were even more discredited then than now. Only in this present decade is there sufficient understanding, in a few chosen minds, to appreciate properly the ancient life of the North, and sufficient courage to dare to state to the world the cause of the long blight and the remedy provided in the knowledge Iceland so generously yields.

Were it not for the recuperative power of nature, always savouring of the miraculous, there would be little hope of the recovery of the human race from eighteen hundred years of Christianity. As Dr. Oswald says, and his words cannot be too often repeated: "The night of the Middle Ages was not the natural blindness of unenlightened barbarians, but an unnatural darkness, maintained by an elaborate system of spiritual despotism, and in spite of the fierce struggles of many light-loving nations." To this is due our mixed ideas of right and wrong, our confusion when we are forced to any moral step, our dependence on authorities, our vacillation, our utter lack of self-reliance. Pride is not in a man's own conscious sense of worth, of honour, of bravery, but in externals; money is his glory and defence. He cannot trust himself, nor, from his knowledge of himself, is he inclined to trust or love others. What reason has he to suppose them any better than himself? Policy rules him, why should it not rule them? He has his master, and he knows it; the Church owns him; with the little remaining intelligence he possesses he knows that the Church owns all, except the unbelievers, and these are dangerous company. Even if the truth is with these persons, which he is not quite clear-headed enough to decide—and after all is there any such thing as truth?—he is not willing to relinquish the benefits the Church doles out to him for the sake of any fanatical notions of following one's convictions.

Max Nordau, in his "Conventional Modern Lies," describes this mental state well: "The conflict between the new view of life and the old institutions rages in the soul of every cultured person, and each and all long to flee from this inner tumult. It is now believed in many quarters, that there are two methods of regaining the lost soul's-peace and that one has a free choice between availing one's self of one or the other. Resolute retrogression one is called, resolute advance the other. Either one gives the forms that have lost their substance this substance back again, or one tears them down completely and gets them out of the way." He elaborates this idea very skilfully, demonstrating that there is really no middle course: one must either revive mediævalism, or sweep all mediæval institutions from the earth. "These are the two methods," he concludes, "and the adherents of the first combat those of the other, and their desperate conflicts constitute the only contents of the political and mental life of the age." There is even more under this conflict than he indicates: it is the unceasing effort of the Romish Church, even through the channels of Protestantism, to regain its lost dominion, to bring back the Middle Ages upon the earth. Whatever the dissatisfaction of the victims during those deplorable ages, the Church had no complaint to make, and paganism, the Reformation, science, rationalism, republicanism, are all forms of one and the same apostasy, which it is the business of the Church to stop, once and for ever. It is plain that this apostasy has reached its worst stage in America, and that in the United States, which, in the framing of their Constitution, have given such a mortal affront to the Church, the battle must be fought out. It is not to be supposed for an instant that Americans will repudiate science, rationalism, and republicanism; they are already more liberal than they know; the only mistake has been that they have not yet realized the discrepancy between loyalty to the Constitution and loyalty to the Christian religion, and that only a monarchist of Europe, devoted to all the old institutions, can be a true Christian. The hour is approaching that will reveal to Americans the untenable position they have attempted to hold, and the immediate occasion for discussion upon the subject is the question of the relative claims of Columbus and the Norse discoverers to American recognition.

The decision of the people of this Republic will thus turn

the scale, one way or the other. The recognition of Columbus' claims, and homage paid to him as the discoverer, signifies approval of the Christian motives and policy since their incipiency; it is to accept as genuine garbled and mutilated history, to exalt a pretender to the highest honour. The recognition of the claims of the Norse discoverers is to show forcibly and conclusively that national integrity, at this present day, consists in paying the highest respect to historical truth, and in honouring those who have transmitted it to posterity, pure and complete; it consists in attributing the greatest blessings enjoyed by civilized nations, liberty, general intelligence, personal rights, just and equitable laws, to the true sources of these. To follow the bidding of the Church and celebrate Columbus' deed were to commit a ridiculous and irretrievable blunder, while to celebrate the Norse achievement would retrieve at a single stroke all the blunders of the past and inaugurate a new era.

However firmly the foundations of the Church are laid upon a future life, all its creeds and dogmas being based on salvation or the reverse, its doctrine and theory one of postponement,— the *action* of the Church has ever been materialistic, bent on immediate results of the most tangible and advantageous kind; in other words, the benefits to be derived from the Christian religion were, to the votaries, relinquishment of actual advantages for long-deferred ones; to Church dignitaries and officials, the appropriation of present advantages without reference to the future heaven. The poor devotees and zealots needed heaven; or were made to believe that they did; the Church needed landed estates, money, temporal power, followers, subjugated nations, and to secure these has been its only object. Preaching heaven, it prized earth! But for the idea of heaven, it could not have spoliated and plundered all the people of the earth. This has been the practical use of Bible, creed, and Christ! If this has been the ecclesiastical policy all through the Middle Ages, it is equally the policy pursued still in Europe and the United States, and will be until religious brigandage is suppressed by the law of nations.

As far as the Scandinavian North was concerned, the Romish purpose is again indicated in the following paragraph from Fryxell's "Narratives from Swedish History:" "At this period Swedish, Norwegian, and Danish Vikings swarmed throughout the whole of Southern Europe, and caused universal dismay by their plundering and marauding. It was therefore determined at several Church Councils to attempt the conversion of these heathen people to Christianity, and by softening their manners and feelings, put an end to their murder and bloodshed." Thus conversion, forced conversion of these people, was purely a prudential measure on the part of the Church; the only way, moreover, in which the plundered property could be made to change hands. As for "softening their manners and feelings, and putting an end to their murder and bloodshed," we can take the two Christianized kings, Olof Tryggvason and Olof the Saint, not to speak of the Swedish king, Olof Skötkonung, and their Christianizing processes, as shining examples of this! Olof Tryggvason declared that "he would either bring it to this, that all Norway should be Christian, or die." It is said of him that "he was distinguished for cruelty when he was enraged, and tortured many of his enemies"—of course all pagans were his enemies;—"some he burnt in fire; some he had torn in pieces by mad dogs; some he had mutilated, or cast down from high precipices." Olof the Saint propagated "the doctrine of mildness and peace," in the same way: "He also made the laws to be read there as elsewhere, by which the people are commanded to observe Christianity; and he threatened every man with loss of life, and limbs, and property, who would not subject himself to Christian law. He inflicted severe punishments on many men, great as well as small, and left no district until the people had consented to adopt the holy faith."

Prescott remarks that "many a bloody page of history attests the fact, that fanaticism, armed with power, is the sorest evil which can befall a nation." If we substitute Christianity for fanaticism, the words will have precisely the same force, and, indeed, the proselyting work throughout has been much more characterized by cold-blooded calculation than by burning zeal. The same author also says: "Acts of intolerance are to be discerned from the earliest period in which Christianity became the established religion of the Roman Empire." Llorente, in tracing the origin of the Inquisition, leads directly to the fact that cruelty, torture, and murder were the earliest means used for the subduing of heretics or heathen: "This first step, which the popes and bishops had taken contrary to the doctrine of St. Paul, was the principle and origin of the Inquisition; for when the custom of punishing a heretic by corporeal pain, although he was a good subject, was once established, it became necessary to vary the punishments, to augment their number, to render them more or less severe, according to the character of each sovereign, and to regulate the manner of prosecuting the culprit." A strange institution, this, for softening manners and feelings, and putting an end to murder and bloodshed! It is estimated by Llorente that Ferdinand and Isabella, through their cruel measures, lost two millions of subjects. "If any sect," says Ludvig Börne, "should ever take it into their heads to worship the devil in his distinctive qualities, and devote themselves to the promotion of human misery in all its forms, the catechism of such a religion could be found ready-made in the code of several monastic colleges." Lecky affirms that in almost every country the abolition of torture was at last effected by a movement which the Church opposed, and by men whom she had cursed.

Hence it appears that torture, extreme bodily suffering and death, were methods inseparable from the constitution of Christianity; its theory was—salvation obtained under extreme difficulty beyond; its practice—exemption from torture, bodily suffering or death, only secured by entire concession to the demands of the Church. These demands, invariably, were for *gain ;* the Church gave spiritual nothings, the most vague and false of promises, in return for substantial property: it grew rich in exact proportion as its converts were impoverished ; pretending to have the monopoly of heaven, it actually gained the monopoly of earth and has kept it in every land called Christian. A little further light will be thrown upon the theological method by these words of Lecky's : " Now, of all systems the world has ever seen, the philosophies of ancient Greece and Rome appealed most strongly to the sense of virtue, and Christianity to the sense of sin." The Church was well aware at the start that unless men and women could be forced to confess themselves sinners, could be overcome with a sense of their own abasement, they would not tamely yield up the goods and possessions that the Church coveted. He adds : " The ideal of the first was the majesty of self-relying humanity ; the ideal of the other was the absorption of the manhood into God." The ideal of the ancient Scandinavians was the same as that of the ancient Greeks and Romans: the majesty of self-relying humanity, and it was chiefly this that stood in the way of Christian purposes.

Enough has been seen and known of the deeds of the Church ; it only remains to connect these deeds with their motive and to judge the Church accordingly. No enlightened nation has ever denied that the deeds were evil, but all have maintained strenuously that the motives for the deeds were pure and high, and that the Church, on the whole, has been justified in pursuing the course it has. Therein lies the fatal error. The action of the Romish Church and of the entire Christian Church, prior to the Reformation, is epitomized in the use it has made of the two discoveries of America, and its treatment of the discoverers. This apparent episode is the pivot upon which all history has turned, and the bulk of past events resolve into this single long, intense drama! In the Columbus claim the whole motive of the Church stands revealed, its boundless cupidity and avarice! Its crimes are all of the nature of those that the laws of civilized countries punish most severely, inasmuch as all infringements of the rights of property are considered the grossest offences; under the head of dishonesty, come robbery, spoliation, plunder, marauding, and depredations of every kind; of all of these the Church is guilty, *for it uses violent means, uses threats, to obtain money.* Every sending-out of missionaries to the heathen is a marauding expedition, all of the intimidations of the priests and clergymen are to the end of robbery, every threat of hell is ruffianism, to secure plunder. These organized robbers, of whom the whole civilized world stand in awe, who enjoy complete immunity, could not gain a stiver from those they oppress, except through inspiring fear.

It is this system of intimidation that the United States, together with the nations of Europe, is tacitly sanctioning, but the Roman Catholic Church is not content with this. All these crimes have been perpetrated before by the Church and perpetrated with impunity, but in insisting on the recognition of Columbus' claims, the Church demands from the United States, and from the world, *public* sanction of these crimes and permission to continue them. It demands, furthermore, the ratification of the Act of Pope Alexander VI., in deeding the continent, of which the American Republic now forms a part, to Spain, by means of a voluntary surrender of that coveted land, in the excess of its gratitude to the man and the power to whom it is said to owe all its greatness,—its voluntary surrender to the Holy See in Rome!

But there is a double movement to effect the end desired: simultaneously with the persuasions used in the Columbus matter, is the coercion of a set of men, under the control of the Catholic Church and in complete harmony with its purposes, known as the Home Rule party. The leaders of this party employ threats that revive the recollection of the early days of Christianity, so violent and brutal are they. They have distinctly proclaimed that there is no extreme that they will not resort to, to force England and the United States to accede to their demands. And what are these demands? The wholesale adoption of the Roman Catholic faith? Not thus expressed; the demands are for Home Rule in Ireland, and the so-called Liberal portion of an unthinking and heedless public do not discern that inasmuch as Ireland is mainly Roman Catholic, Home Rule for a large Roman Catholic majority means no more nor less than *Roman Catholic rule in Ireland*, the wielding of almost unrestricted political power by the most unscrupulous of Jesuitical demagogues; it means the establishment of a Roman Catholic seat and stronghold, west of England and north of France, that can harass both, drawing its chief sustenance from the great nation across the Atlantic, which hordes of Irish-American allies are using all their infernal arts to subvert to their foul purposes and which they confidently believe will yield to these arts and become the future empire of the Pope; it means the elevation of Papal power to a high northern latitude, for the first time since the Reformation; it means converting the Irish race, hitherto the scum of the earth, into the scourge of the earth, to harass and torment all the other nations.

These are the full dimensions of the plot, the double plot, connected by a subterranean passage of chicanery. If either succeeds, the Columbus attempt, or the Home Rule attempt, it is equivalent to having both succeed, for the Irish Catholic party will win the day. And success, as they confidently boast, depends only on the amount of coercion they use. As of old, they have no scruple about the means; the slaughter of thousands of innocent persons, butchery, rapine, the firing or blowing-up of cities, savagery in every form, it is the old programme re-enacted, and goes to show how utterly impervious Roman Catholics, the most devout and faithful of all Christians, are **to** all civilizing and humanizing influences. After a life of several years in the United States, amid American institutions, they come out as perfect types of mediævalism as if born and bred in Spain or Italy, and are ready to lay their sacrilegious hands on the fairest and noblest productions of civilization. In their thought, England and the United States are already doomed. To such a height has the avarice of the Romish Church reached!

Like a prophecy of succour from the impending evil come these words: " From the depths of the North—from a remote and unknown island—a dawning light appeared, the harbinger of a bright day that was to enlighten the Scandinavian North for a century to come, and to extend its rays through other lands and down to later ages." From this North we know that reason has once reigned; we know how the reign ceased, and we discern dimly how we can cause its renewal.

It would now become a work of supererogation to specify the beneficial results of according to Iceland its full due, of emulating its freedom and enlightenment during the days when it was a flourishing republic, and before it became Christianized,— of attributing the discovery of America to the dauntless men who sailed from those Northern shores. The North failed and sank into a decline through accepting Christianity; the treasured records of its experience are revealed to the two nations at present so grievously threatened by the rallying power of Rome, England and the American Republic, just in time to save them from its grasp. But for the history handed down to us from Iceland, we could not have known the extent of the evil the Church has wrought, for we would have had no uncontaminated race, morally sound and healthy, to compare with the diseased and enfeebled one the Church has produced. The actual life in Iceland, the intellectual stature of its people, reveal to us undreamed-of possibilities. In casting off the incubus of the Church we do not enter unguardedly into vague and problematical conditions, but we resume conditions once found all-sufficient for human welfare, we will again lead the life of rational beings, and defamed reason will be our one sure guide.

After the defeat of its present plans the Church of Rome will hardly be in a position to repeat its efforts for the ruin of mankind. Thanks to Iceland, and the chronicles of the Scandinavian North, the Church now suffers exposure as well as defeat, and its true nature will for the first time become known. Henceforth, however repulsive, it will cease to be a dangerous power.

VIEW AT THINGVALLA.

CHAPTER X.

THE CELEBRATION OF IT IN 1985!

ICELAND and the United States have several points in common and their fate is interwoven : they were first settled by men of the same race; both have been republics, and it will stand recorded in history that both have had a Millennial Celebration. "And an American," says Samuel Kneeland, "could not fail to admire the courage of these old Norsemen, and to feel pity for their subsequent loss of liberty; and the more, as Iceland and New England are, as far as I know, the only two great republics founded on a love of civil and religious liberty, free from the sordid motives of love of gain and power." He asserts that Iceland was justified in proclaiming to the nations the celebration of her one thousandth anniversary, and the parallel between the two will be maintained in this respect also, for the American Republic will not only be justified in proclaiming to the world the celebration of the one thousandth anniversary of its discovery by the Norsemen, but impelled by every high motive to pay this tribute to them and to Iceland!

In this celebration, one hundred years hence, Iceland will renew its youth; in this it will reap the reward of its long labours for the American Republic, urged to this public act by the force, of truth, by a deep sense of all that it owes to the mother republic, will then be Iceland's handiwork, the flowering-out of the ancient wisdom so richly stored there! Ere Americans can have this celebration, they must take the step that will for the first time make them a free nation, they must abolish spiritual slavery as effectually as they have abolished the physical; there must be another declaration of independence, this time against the Church of Rome and its tributary; there must be another declaration of emancipation,—the temples and their sacraments regarded as so many slave-marts, where *souls* are bought and sold; the property of the slave-owners must be confiscated. And one hundred years after this has been done, one hundred years of development and progress, under the most favourable conditions a nation has ever enjoyed, with the sense of having achieved the grandest triumph in the world's history, the utter extinction of idolatry,—the United States will be prepared to have a celebration of unequalled grandeur!

To attempt to describe now, while we are yet in spiritual bondage, while the United States yet bears the spiritual lineaments of the Old World, and knows of liberty only in the rudimentary sense, what such a celebration could be would lead one to be accused of the most wildly utopian views; any description would partake of the fabulous! Such a thing as a state of society based on the positive knowledge that *will is might* and that a rightly directed will is the omnipotent factor for good, is absolutely inconceivable for the people of this generation, in their impotency and flaccidity. Now they will not exert themselves, because they believe exertion useless, and this has palsied them; then they will not need to exert themselves, for their natural strength, of body and mind, will be so great that everything they do will seem easy to them. They will wonder in those happy days, not so far distant, how there could ever have been poverty in the United States, when the Church has been made to disgorge and the wealth locked up in ecclesiastical establishments has been evenly distributed; how there could ever have been starvation, when the rich soil yields so bountifully; how there could ever have been mental famine, a paucity of ideas, when the mind yields thoughts as abundantly as the soil yields fruits and grains, and one is no longer baffled with social problems. Then human beings will realize that the earth was made to live in, that it is adapted to their highest needs, and that, whatever the next world may have to offer, satisfaction is not to be postponed until reaching it. If we have made the progress we have under a totally mistaken idea of existence, what will be our advancement when a happy and reliable theory takes the place of the present absurdly dismal one? What will be the sensations of those permanently released from the Church cell? How will the world seem to them when there is no more regulation-diet, no more seventh-day rites, no more Bible prescriptions and monotonous reading from a gloomy book that has become the chief infliction of civilized life? How will the heavens look, when the Church canopy that has hidden the heavens from human gaze is removed? How will the earth look, when the Church curse is taken off of it? How will men and women appear, when they for the first time look each other in the face and see no brand there? Yes, the time will come when people will have no sorrow save the stinging recollection that they could ever have been such perverse, sickly fools in the past!

New-found health and joy, the recovered use of human powers, will in themselves be a celebration, but good inward conditions never fail of producing brilliant outward results and supply materials for that which will dazzle the eye and intoxicate the senses. It will be a duty, moreover, on that transcendent occasion, to show that a great nation, like the United States, does not depend upon the Church to produce splendid effects or to arrange a festival on a scale of princely magnificence!

Part of the celebration at Iceland was held at Thingvalla, on the Mount of Laws, the very spot where the ancient *Things* were held, " during the palmy days of the young and flourishing Iceland Republic,—during the four centuries of its independence and remarkable intellectual vigour." These *Things* were established there in 928 and in 1800 removed to Reikiavik. Our celebration might take place along the whole Atlantic coast discovered and explored by the Northmen, from Labrador to Florida, and in the next one hundred years the free institutions of which the ancient *Things* were the germ, will render those shores glorious in the extreme! The progress of the last two hundred years has been retarded by Puritanism, witch-hunts, the persecution of the Quakers, and Quaker conservatism, slave-hunts, the war for independence and the war for emancipation, the clamour for rights and justice from slaves, women, the working-classes—and authors. Somehow with the emigrants to America, all the old evils had emigrated too, and sought freedom to exercise themselves. They were tenacious, these evils, and hard to eradicate. Puritanism still remains; if that could have been eradicated *first*, the whole train of evils would have been removed with it. As it was, Americans left that unmolested, and have had to grapple with each of the social problems in turn : the slavery question, the woman question, the temperance question, the labour question, the finance question, settling but one of them in these two centuries—the slavery question. Social economists and reformers are tugging away at each of the social evils, honestly deploring them, but really nourishing them through this allegiance to the Church. What is needed is manhood : too much manhood to oppress, too much manhood to endure oppression; too much manhood to offer liquor, too much manhood to drink it ; too much manhood to treat women badly, or as inferiors, too much womanhood, which is the same in essence, to put up with ill-treatment or to accept an inferior position. The Church has destroyed self-respect ; hence these evils. They are the direct result of Christian preaching. Poverty is not caused by lack of money, but its appropriation in large quantities by those authorized by the Church to be rulers and masters, ecclesiastics of all grades, of which the Pope is head, sovereigns, state officials, capitalists, employers; the rest may fare as best they can.

In the Iceland Republic none of these reforms were needed, unless, perhaps, the vice of intemperance could have been abated. We have been told repeatedly by Christian writers that the introduction of Christianity in the North did away with slavery. If this is true, why did the northern states of the American Union have to wage a fierce war with the southern states for the suppression of an institution which the Church, calling it divine, fully supported; nay, which the Church, through its good servants, the Spanish monarchs and Columbus, had introduced and promoted? Mallet gives Christianity the credit of having "re-established a part of mankind, who groaned under a miserable slavery, in their natural rights," but there is no evidence of this in the sagas; on the contrary, there is a vehement protest from many a fearless and outspoken pagan against the slavery that the priests and kings were attempting to put upon them, the bondage of the new faith, and Laing asserts that "in Norway this class (the slaves) appear to have been better treated than on the south side of the Baltic and to have had some rights. Lodin had to ask his slave Astrid to accept of him in marriage. . . . One owner, Erling Skialgsson, gave them land to sow, and gave them the benefit of their own crops; and he put upon them a certain value, so that they could redeem themselves from slavery, which some could do the first or second year, and 'all who had any luck could do it in the third year.'" From this it appears that slavery already existed in the Christian countries on the south side of the Baltic, and consequently could not have offended the religious sense of the missionaries and priests when they travelled northward. Oswald expresses the plain truth by saying: "The Church that abolished slavery in name promoted it in fact; for her doctrine implied a divine sanction of despotism, and an entire disregard for man's natural rights. The slave-barracks of ancient Rome were temples of liberty compared with the dungeons of the hierarchical torture-dens, where thousands of nature's noblemen vainly invoked death and madness as a refuge from the power of a more cruel foe."

A continuation of the slave-system is the poverty-curse. The poor have no rights, and they are considered to be bound for life. A hireling is a slave to all intents and purposes; labour and the labourer are equally despised; the favoured upper classes all over Europe and the United States hold the belief that the working-class are born solely to toil for them and to minister to their comfort; this servitude is to be their permanent state, and they have no right to resist it or to aspire beyond it. Their wages are the least amount that they can possibly subsist on; education, leisure, enjoyment, opportunity, the use of their higher faculties, are denied them; they are regarded as a species of domestic animal, whose muscles are of the only value to the community. Artisans and mechanics are a grade higher, but are likewise condemned to routine work, have closely stipulated exactions laid upon them, and are debarred from privileges.

The sum-total of the wrongs and injustice suffered by women, including that monster evil prostitution, is to be traced directly to the Bible, to the gross impurity of all the ideas contained in that book regarding marriage, the conjugal relation, procreation, woman's nature. Pretending to worship the Creator, to revere his revealed work, creation, the Bible pronounces the highest function delegated to the human species, procreation, *vile,* an act instigated by the lowest, most bestial carnal desire, and the human race are invariably spoken of as "conceived in sin." This is the reason why Jesus Christ was an ascetic and celibate, and why this unnatural way of life was alone deemed holy and exemplary. Marriage could only be hallowed by making it a sacrament, and was respectable and decent only because it was a bond for life. The Church recognizes in marriage nothing but a sexual relation; it is the legalizing of passion; hence it is opposed to divorce, which at once places man and woman on a higher footing with each other, inferring intellectual companionship, reciprocity of thought and feeling, and liberty of choice. It is conceded to be the duty of moral beings, in every other respect, to retract a wrong course and to repair any blunder they may have committed; in the matter of marriage the Church forbids this. But in the Scandinavian North, before Bible or creed were accepted, or the Galilean god set up for worship, marriage was contracted without any religious ceremony and could be dissolved for any just and sufficient cause.

Oswald observes: "We have been taught to treat the body as an enemy of the soul; and, if bodily health is an obstacle to true saintliness, we have evidently progressed in the path of salvation." But the Norsemen honoured the body, developed it to the highest possible perfection, and in the sagor and "Heimskringla" one frequently reads of some king or warrior, that he was extremely handsome, large and well-formed, while great praise is given to the beauty of the Northern women. Sickliness and weakness were despised among them, and no death was more ignominious for a man than that on a sick-bed. Their theories were the reverse of those held in these modern times in every respect. "Sublunary life," says Oswald, "according to a still prevalent theory, is a state of probation for testing a man's power of self-denial." Where the Christians relinquished, the Norsemen grasped; and in their grand self-expansion, acknowledging no limits, no prohibitions, they fairly imbibed greatness from their surroundings, visible and invisible, and absorbed the power of the elements into themselves; essentially spiritual in their mentality they paid all deference to qualities, analyzed these, and arriving at accurate conclusions as to what was worthy of high-minded men, they accorded to themselves the true place in the scale of being and took their place, proudly and defiantly, as the lords of creation, in a literal sense. The modern, or Christian world, has been divided in opinion as to whether mankind were born to rule, or to be ruled, but this ancient race did not even debate the question, they knew instinctively that men were born to rule, and they did rule.

It is necessary for Americans to come back to this knowledge, and having acted upon it for a hundred years, they will be qualified to celebrate the anniversary in question in a spirit worthy of their Norse progenitors! The evils that the American people are vainly striving to reform, disabled as they are by the palsying conviction that all human effort is well-nigh unavailing, are manifestly not derived from any Norse ethics. These, on the contrary, have been the source of infinite good, as demonstrated by scores of authors, and destined to be demonstrated with overwhelming force when all the philosophy and wisdom stored up in the historic records of the North shall have been published to the world; but let us look on the reverse side of the picture and note, with Oswald, what the effect has been of the Christian doctrines. "Have they ever added one millet-seed to the sum of human happiness?" he asks. "Did the apostle of Nazareth ever speak one word in favour of industry, of rational education, the cause of health, the love and study of nature, of physical and intellectual culture? Not one. Has he promoted our progress in the paths of science and freedom? Not one step."

It will be difficult, therefore, to assign any good reason for further adherence to these doctrines. To tear down Christianity, under present conditions, is in no wise iconoclasm; neither will it leave a moral vacuum; the necessity is not even upon us of building up something else in its stead, for a structure has stood for ages, testified to by reliable history, which the Church and Christianity have obscured and hidden from the gaze; we need engage in no useless or doubtful experimenting, for a republic, carried on under rationalistic principles, has once existed, and will serve as a model for the reconstruction of modern commonwealths. A republic is but half a republic, if with a free constitution, the inhabitants of the land submit to the Christian despotism, being subjects of the Church, and in reality are governed through fear, the fear of future punishment. Through the Church, monarchy, in its worst form, is maintained in the United States. Through the Church, mediævalism, with all its vices and corruption, is maintained; and so long as this is the case, nothing approaching to a modern state of society can be obtained.

Lest the enthusiasm roused by the anticipation of the grandest celebration on record, in 1985, be chilled by the thought that it is one hundred years off, and that the present generation, and even the next, will not live to see it, it should be borne in mind that such a celebration cannot be accomplished in a day or a generation. If we would have it in any degree a worthy one, we must begin now. Seeds must be sown for such a harvest as that! Iceland, in celebrating her millennial, had a thousand years' life to show, in which she had done more than any other commonwealth "for liberty, the advance of knowledge, and the preservation of historic records, at a time when the rest of Europe was in darkness," but the American Republic has done nothing as yet to earn the distinction that fate has reserved for it in this millennial, which at once invests the young nation, lacking ancestral dignity, with an antiquity dating a thousand years back, and one that has heretofore been the mere spoils of an Italian adventurer and an avaricious ecclesiastical hierarchy—with the honour of having been discovered by worthy and independent men, led to its shores by no sordid motives. The glory of this fact wipes out the ignominy of the other. But as yet the people of the United States have not even acknowledged this fact; several of the leading American historians deny it. The adherents of one historic party are pressing Columbus' claims; the adherents of the other have not effectually set these aside. There has been no proclamation of the truth, and the public at large are so utterly unaware of it that they still hold to the pious tradition that Columbus discovered America, in 1492.

The first duty is obviously to confirm the fact of the Norse discovery; the second, to make all the history so miraculously preserved in Iceland accessible, through translation and publication, to the entire English-speaking public; the third, is for this same public to endeavour to emulate the glorious example of their ancestors. It were not wise to predict that more than this can be done in a hundred years. But if less is done, the American Republic will not be prepared to celebrate the millennial anniversary of its discovery as it should be celebrated!

INTERIOR OF THE ANTIQUARIAN MUSEUM, REYKJAVIK.

CHAPTER XI.

THE RIGHTED POSITION OF THE SCANDINAVIAN NORTH AFTER THIS JUSTICE HAS BEEN ACCORDED TO IT.

In the single statement that the discovery of America by the Norsemen has never been conceded by the world to be a fact, is comprised the universal injustice that has been done the Scandinavian North. By the Scandinavian North is meant definitely: Sweden, Norway, Denmark, and Iceland; thus four nations that have individually and collectively sustained the most brilliant national *rôle* that has ever been acted in Europe, or in the world, have been wilfully consigned to obscurity, their history concealed or distorted. Should it be asked, How has this been possible, and why have they allowed it? the answer is, that their strength was sapped by the introduction of Christianity, *planned and carried out solely for this purpose;* that the whole of Catholic Europe has been in combination against them, first as pagans, then as Protestants; and that the assumption of Christian humility and weakness so completely destroyed their ancient pride that they were not capable of reasserting themselves and gaining their former rank.

The world has rung with the exploits of great generals and conquerors, with the names of Alexander the Great, Hannibal, Napoleon, Wellington; but Hastings, Rolf, Ragnar Lodbrok's sons, Harold Hårfager, William the Conqueror, Canute, are scarcely heard of; nevertheless, England was twice conquered by Norse kings, and even the great King Alfred was compelled to divide the land with the followers of Odin. When other rulers have engaged in wars of conquest, this has redounded to their glory, and superior statesmanship, valour, ambition, generalship, have been accorded to them; when the Norsemen have engaged in wars of conquest, achieving unparalleled victories, these results have been described as the ravages of lawless depredators, the incursions of the Northern sea-robbers, of the piratical Danes, &c., &c. Military life, adjudged honourable and justifiable, to this day, by all civilized nations, was, when pursued by them, alleged to be an evidence of their ferocity and barbarism. With bolder and more far-reaching plans for attaining the supremacy of Europe than even Russia has ever indulged in, the Scandinavians were represented as men of limited intelligence only equal to pillaging expeditions against unprotected coasts. The Spaniards, too, have been quite willing to forget this little episode which occurred in the ninth century: "From Gaul the Northmen crossed to Spain (A.D. 827), where they came in contact with the Arab conquerors, and penetrated as far as Seville, the fortifications of which they demolished. The votaries of Odin prevailed over those of Mohammed; and proceeding southward, they passed the outlet of the Mediterranean, which from its resemblance to their own Baltic Strait, they called the Niærva Sund, or the Narrow Sound." This is contained in "Scandinavia, Ancient and Modern," by Andrew Crichton and Henry Wheaton. They also penetrated to Jerusalem, literally scouring the earth, and concerning such cosmopolites such a statement as that in Cooley's "History of Maritime and Inland Discovery," namely, that "the geographical knowledge possessed by the Northern nations was never circumscribed within such narrow limits as those which confined the views of the early inhabitants of Greece and Italy,"—finds ready credence with those who have begun the study of this remarkable race. Among the cultured inhabitants of all modern nations are very many very expert travellers, who have produced a voluminous literature respecting the foreign countries they have visited, and yet these would be simply dazed and bewildered in reading of the way in which the Norsemen travelled, the distance traversed,—time and space both annihilated,—the ease with which they transported fleets, armies, from one part of the world to another. In the "Heimskringla" one may read, hit or miss, of almost any one of the Norwegian kings, Harold Hårfager, Hakon, Olaf Tryggvason, or Olaf the Saint, and find that he goes over to Sweden to have a consultation with the Swedish king, looks into Denmark to see how things are getting on there, travels back and forth from Nidaros, the Throndhjem of the high North, to the Romsdal or southern Norway, or Ringerike, sails around the dreaded promontory Stad, the terror of all modern mariners, without the slightest difficulty, finds time to entertain Icelandic or English visitors, that is, Norsemen from England, to gather the freshest foreign intelligence, and with all this holds survey over the entire Norwegian coast. To one who has travelled over Norway in the nineteenth century, knowing full well the nature of the country and what has to be encountered there, such accounts are simply incredible! It is a slight incident, to be sure, but suggestive, that the ascent of Hornelen, a high and apparently inaccessible mountain, barren of verdure, near Stad, on the west coast, was made by Olaf Tryggvason, who "fixed his shield upon the very peak." One of his followers had also attempted to climb this height, but after awhile could neither get up nor down, so that the king had to go to his rescue and carry him down in his arms. As I have myself twice sailed around Hornelen, I can appreciate all the merits of this exploit! What is still more surprising, there seems to have been no scarcity of food or entertainment in Norway in those days!

There is therefore no exaggeration in the following statement, also by Wheaton: "In perusing the relation of their extraordinary achievements, we are impressed with the familiar recollection, that it is the history of a race not only sprung from the same lineage, but, in former times, our superiors in the arts both of war and peace." More than the conquest of nations, the Norsemen completed the conquest over themselves; their heroism has never been surpassed; it is related that Ragnar Lodbrok died singing, and Saxo records, as the greatest praise of a celebrated champion, that "he fell, laughed, and died."

And yet it is the history of this race that has been suppressed! Could the envy and malice of their Christian inferiors have been carried farther? And what is the result? The people of Europe and the United States are very nearly as ignorant of the Scandinavian North and its inhabitants, of its degree of culture, its customs, as if Sweden, Norway and Denmark were situated at the base of the Himalayas! Indeed, the two first, especially, are supposed to be encompassed in Siberian darkness and snow. They are ostracized from other nations almost as roving tribes are debarred from intercourse with settled inhabitants; there is a lingering echo of "roving freebooters" in the refined mind, and to make the acquaintance of a cultivated Scandinavian is deemed a very piquant and unusual experience for a lady or gentleman of society. The language that was once "the court language in Norway, Sweden, Denmark, England, and at Rouen, became confined to Iceland, and its two offshoots, the Danish and Swedish tongues were, together with the parent-tongue, soon forgotten in England, and in later centuries have seldom been learned by any foreigner." The early history of Europe is thus locked up in an unknown language, or to speak definitely, the history of Russia, Switzerland, Italy, Normandy, Great Britain, the Orkney and Shetland Isles, Iceland, Norway, Sweden, and Denmark! Catholic Germany and France, Italy, and Spain have been able consequently to suppress all knowledge of the ancient life and culture of the greater part of Europe! It is permissible here to again cite Wilhelmi's statement that "in the

Heimskringla we obtain from the narratives of the Icelanders' extensive voyages through all Europe to Rome, Constantinople and Jerusalem, also the knowledge of the history, geography and antiquity of eastern, western and southern Europe." Fortunately, the "Heimskringla" is translated and accessible to the entire English-reading public, but there are tomes upon tomes of history that are not translated; the extent of this can be judged of somewhat from the fact that there is a catalogue in existence, containing the names of two hundred and thirty of the most distinguished scalds, from the ninth century until the reign of Waldemar II., and the scalds and sagamen, be it remembered, were the historians of the North. It is affirmed by Cooley that "the Scandinavians and the Arabians, are perhaps the only people among whom the reading or recital of histories ever became the ordinary amusement;" this was the superb fruit of the Norsemen's cultivation of the art of peace.

The first era of discovery was that inaugurated by the Norse voyagers, who found coast after coast; the second was the quest for Icelandic manuscripts, in which discoveries, conquests, all manner of achievements were recorded; it was the discovery of historical records; this, too, was Norse, or Scandinavian; the vague knowledge that there were such records in existence did not stimulate England or France to search for the annals of their own ancestors; this was left to Denmark, with the active assistance of the Icelanders. Among the latter, Arngrim Jónsson is mentioned as the man "who stands at the head of the restorers of learning in Iceland." It was he who discovered the prose Edda, in 1628. Another Icelander, Brynjúlf Sveinsson, found fragments of both the prose and poetic Edda, and, in the year 1640, found the poetic Edda complete. This information is contained in the introduction to "The Religion of the Northmen," by Professor Rudolph Keyser. From the same source we learn that "the government also took an active interest in these antiquarian researches. In 1662, Frederick III. sent Torfæus to Iceland to collect manuscripts, and in 1685 Christain V. forbade the sale of them to any foreigner." Sweden was also very active in these researches, and the names of many distinguished antiquaries do the country honour. The antiquarian archives were established at Upsala, according to the same authority, as early as 1669, and in 1692 removed to Stockholm; their object was the preservation of Runic monuments and Icelandic manuscripts.

The knowledge contained in these Icelandic manuscripts is as indispensable to the English and Americans as to the people of the North, yet they do not have it and they scarcely know the writers on Scandinavian mythology and ancient history, Suhm, Schöning, P. E. Müller, Lgaerbring, Peringskiöld, Nyerup, Grundtvig, Montelius, Hildebrand, Thorlacius, Finn Magnussen, even by name. Of modern Scandinavian history they know very nearly as little. The characters of Gustaf Adolf and Carl XII., to be sure, loom up out of the mist that enshrouds Scandinavia, and among artists and authors, Frederika Bremer, Jenny Lind, Thorwaldsen, Hans Christian Andersen, Tegnér, are regarded as phenomena as rare as they are wonderful. The presence of such men in Paris as August Hagborg, Hugo Salmson, Normann, Smith-Hald, Heyerdahl, Wahlberg, is just beginning to be acknowledged in art; Walter Runeberg is becoming celebrated as a sculptor, but the works of his father, the greatest poet who ever wrote in the Swedish tongue, have with two exceptions, a volume of his lyrics and "Nadeschda,"[1] never been translated into English. It is quite sufficient to concede that Sweden has produced one poet, Tegnér; Runeberg, Geijer, Nicander, Wallin, von Braun, Bellman, Malmström, Böttiger, Snoilsky, can remain in ob-

[1] The first by Eiríkr Magnússon and E. H. Palmer, the second by Marie A. Brown.

scurity. In the library of the Göteborg Museum, the works on Swedish history fill seventy-one pages of the catalogue, and doubtless a proportionate number of the shelves; one can find there about everything, from the early writings of Ericus Olai, and of Johannes Messenius, in Latin, to those of Mellin, Geijer, Fryxell, Starbäck, Afzelius, and the rest; their name is legion; but so long as Sweden's history is not admitted to be a constituent part of the world's history, it matters but little who its historians are.

At the present practical juncture the lack of all this knowledge is a very serious drawback to right action; it will be found that instead of slighting insignificant countries, unworthy the attention of cultured English and Americans, these have been debarring themselves from that which is most essential to their national development, really cutting themselves off from their best intellectual supplies. They have sought historical knowledge from the wrong sources, and have thus been led away from the truth; this has caused misunderstanding and estrangement between the very nations that ought to have been most closely united and to have felt the deepest pride in their common origin. But this alienation was just what the enemy, the southern Romish enemy, intended; with Norway, Sweden, Denmark, Iceland, England, Scotland, and the United States banded together in the closest fraternity and harmony, as they should be, *and as they will be, once the hidden historical truth becomes known*, Roman Catholic plots and intrigues will stand but a poor chance of success.

There are great numbers of Swedish, Norwegian, and Danish works that ought to be incorporated at once into English literature; among these none would be of more immediate use than the latest history of Sweden, "Sveriges Historia," in six volumes, written by a combination of the most able historians and antiquaries of Sweden, Drs. Montelius and Hildebrand, Professors Alin, Weibull, and others; the style is a highly attractive and popular one, and the work is lavishly illustrated, so richly and intelligently, with scenes and places, historical buildings and relics, antiquities, portraits, the ancient aspects of cities, &c., &c., that the careless and superficial could read the book pictorially, and even in this way gain a better knowledge of Sweden than any persons have possessed before. A paragraph from it will do good service just here, to show the "state of barbarism (?) among the ancient inhabitants of the North." "A visit to the National Museum, and a glance at the gold ornaments there preserved from the middle of the Iron Age, are sufficient to show what an astonishing wealth of gold must have existed here in Sweden 1300 or 1400 years ago. Gold bracelets of a couple of pounds weight are several times found, and not seldom, when one is working in the soil, a large number of gold ornaments are met with from this period, sometimes going up to a considerable weight and a value significant even in our circumstances." The same author, Dr. Oscar Montelius, goes on to say: "Commerce and Viking expeditions, during the period now in question, brought an almost incredible quantity of precious metals, mostly silver, to Sweden. How great the stock of silver at that time was in the land, is best realized by the considerable masses which are still, after the space of about one thousand years, annually dug up from the earth. Only during the last twelve years the National Museum has received more than 72 kilograms (170 pounds!) of silver found in Swedish soil from Viking times. It is remarkable that the silver now appears in such quantity; this metal, it is true, had been known in our land since shortly after the birth of Christ, but for many centuries, clear to the beginning of the Viking period, silver seems to have been more rare here than gold." Describing the large commerce that was sustained, by way of Russia, with the East, he adds: "The certainty is, that Sweden, by way of Russia, obtained from Constantinople costly fabrics and other coveted commodities, which the refined Byzantines had to offer the pomp-loving Northerners in exchange for their valuable furs and other wares." Horace Marryatt states that "in the inventory of Gripsholm, during the reign of King Gustaf, every object noted down is of foreign manufacture." Among the importations during this reign are mentioned dye-stuffs, fruits, garden-products, glass, gold, gems, horses, confectionery, linen wares, silk and velvet, silver, tapestries,—all giving evidence of refinement, love of luxury, and an extremely cultivated taste, and yet the statement that Sweden at the present day has two universities, and upwards of 130 public high and normal schools of various grades, besides the special schools, and 9639 elementary schools; that it has over 4000 miles of railway; a commercial navy of 4411 vessels; a "Sèvres" of its own, the porcelain factory at Rörstrand, which has been the recipient of no less than ten medals, from Paris, Moscow, Berlin, Malimö, Borås, Stockholm, Bogota, Copenhagen, Philadelphia, and Vienna; an opera-house, built by the art-loving Gustaf III., which in 1882 celebrated its centennial, and in which all the operatic requirements, singers, orchestra, ballet, scenic decorations (invariably fine), even to the translation of the text into Swedish, all the Italian librettos, are filled by native artists;—this statement will excite incredulous surprise in all who read it.

The world has been so deeply impressed with the supposed fact of the wretched barbarism and ignorance of the ancient Scandinavians that it stubbornly refuses to believe that the modern Scandinavians have ever made any perceptible progress in letters or art. In England this scepticism is particularly marked; but either there or in the United States the assertion that the contrary is the case, is almost resented. Nevertheless, the *Salon* every year borrows much of its lustre from the works of Scandinavian artists, and such men as Normann, Cederström, Salmson, Hagborg, Smith-Hald, are in no danger of being eclipsed. In Johannes Jaeger's illustrated catalogue of the celebrated art-works of Sweden, Norway and Denmark, there are no less than 618 works, paintings and sculpture included, yet this by no means represents all. These three countries have given their full quota of geniuses to the world, and the general enlightenment would have been immeasurably increased had the fruits of their united labours been accepted. As it is, there has been little or no affiliation between the Scandinavian mind and the European or American mind; the finest literary and art productions of the North have been scorned or ignored altogether; an overwhelming amount of evidence has been required to convince the outside public that the North could produce anything of any value, and these nations, the oldest in civilization and culture, the intellectual parents and teachers of nearly every nation in Europe, have been regarded as tyros, as extremely young and unskilled aspirants for fame, whose mediocrity was only equalled by their presumption in daring to enter the lists at all.

Several centuries of this treatment could not fail to have its effect upon those who suffered it; it has greatly reduced the national sense of greatness in the Scandinavian lands and dimmed the ambition that once burned with so bright a flame. The Swedes of the present day have almost come to believe the world's contemptuous verdict of them; in their wounded feeling their pride now is to be as exclusive as possible and not to seek intercourse with other nations at all; they argue, and with a show of right, "if foreigners are so ignorant as not to estimate us properly, we will make no effort to undeceive them; it is really of no consequence to us what they think." Consequently, although Sweden has acquired a permanent bearing upon the universal mind, a permanent place in the ranks of those who have done most for the advancement of the human race, nay, in respect to securing the fundamental conditions for spiritual enlightenment, even having *led*,—it is suffered to sink into a decline, the records of its past greatness are buried, one cannot say forgotten, for they have never been known, the works of Swedish authors stand, comparatively unread, on the shelves of Swedish libraries, and the country languishes in its isolation, deprived of the prosperity that commerce, large financial relations and extensive intercourse with other lands would yield it. The bulk of the people in Norway are content if a crowd of tourists visit the country every summer simply to view its grand and beautiful scenery. In material development it is not nearly so far advanced as Sweden, is much more thinly populated, and the resources are less in every way. Norway passed into a decline at the expiration of the Viking period, and has nothing in its history to correspond with Sweden's "period of greatness." Still, in its literature and art Norway stands very high, and a few leading spirits among the Norwegians, both at home and abroad, manifest much patriotism and national pride, and in this instance the few will exalt the many. Denmark, however, has steadily held its own, and being greatly favoured by its proximity to the continent, has never been ignored so completely as Norway and Sweden. The Danes have shown more energy and strength of character than the Norwegians and the Swedes, and the steps they have long since taken to demonstrate historic truth in the great matter under consideration, make them the leaders in this new movement.

But whatever remissness the nations of the North may be charged with, the cause of this remissness lies with the other countries, who have almost denied that they existed; and the instigators of this widespread injustice are the Roman Catholics and the Church whence they emanated. The blame for the whole of this disastrous state of things, which must now, in all haste, be changed, to avert a dire calamity, rests upon the people of every land who have acted under Roman Catholic influence and believed Roman Catholic lies, against their better judgment. It is not for these, therefore, to consider the duty of the Norwegians, Danes, and Swedes in the present exigency, but to perform their own. Let them read and ponder well all that has been translated into their respective languages upon Scandinavian history and mythology, and upon the Norse discovery; let them demonstrate and proclaim what they will speedily ascertain to be facts; let them, in a word, turn the tide of error and remove the false landmarks that lead all astray.

One practical step that should be taken at once, is clearly indicated by Professor Howard Crosby in his introductory letter to Sinding's "History of Scandinavia:" "We oddly mingle the old and the new, the dim and the bright, when we turn to Scandinavia, as we do with no other land. This double character naturally lends peculiar attraction to its history. Yet, with all this attraction, the history of no part of Europe is less familiar to the general mind; probably because the Scandinavian countries lie somewhat off from the world's great highways, and participate but moderately in the world's chief commerce. This should not be. The ignorance is a fault, especially among us of English descent, whose ancestral history is so intimately and variously associated with that of Denmark, Sweden and Norway. The Norsemen have left the memorials of their habitation on the coast of Scotland, where Runic inscriptions tell the story of their prowess, while through much of England the familiar names of towns and hamlets are purely Norse. . . . It is therefore full time that our universities should have their chairs of Scandinavian literature, as a needful part of the apparatus for a thorough English education, to render more complete the examination of the roots of our speech and race. While this want is felt, we may gladly hail any contribution to American literature which tends to open this interesting field of research."

Yes, that is precisely what is needed, chairs of Scandinavian literature in the American and English universities, skilful teachers of the Swedish and Danish languages, and a good corps of translators set to work at once to put the most valuable Scandinavian books into English. There should indeed be a society formed to fulfil an office parallel to that of the Royal Society of Northern Antiquaries, in Copenhagen; this society renders the more important of the Icelandic manuscripts accessible to the Danish public, the other should render all valuable Scandinavian histories and records accessible to the entire English-speaking public. This highly necessary work has already been deferred much too long. With every hour that is delayed will the after compunction and humiliation be increased, the painful sense of having defrauded the Scandinavian North of its rightful position, of having been guilty of the basest ingratitude. In the near future it will be realized, too, how deeply we of English descent have defrauded ourselves in defrauding them, how seriously we have lowered our own rank in lowering theirs!

Still, after all remissness and shortcomings, the destiny of the united nations of the Scandinavian stock is a bright one. In a joint act we will both acknowledge our ancestors and be acknowledged as their true heirs and descendants; to give will be to receive in a sense never realized before; once hospitable to Northern thought, Northern history, Northern memories, Northern poetry, to the beauty that Northern genius has evoked from marble and canvas, to the noble legends and traditions that, having done so much to inspire genius in their native realm, will also lead the commercial and materialistic mind of the Continent and the United States to lofty ideals,—once hospitable to these, we will entertain many an angel unawares!

What we are called upon to do, and what we will soon do with glad eagerness, is to attribute to our honoured Norse progenitors the grandest discovery that was ever made, the discovery of the American continent; the conquest and remodelling of nearly the whole of Europe; the founding of several great empires and republics; the manly and determined resistance, for five hundred years, to the system of idolatry known as the Roman Catholic or Christian religion; the renewed opposition to this during the Reformation; the permanent rescue of the three Scandinavian nations, including Iceland, and the American Republic, from the insatiate grasp of the Romish power; the consequent liberty of thought and person.

This done, the Scandinavian North will at once resume its true rank, and stand forth as the acknowledged intellectual and moral leader of the civilized world, as attested by every page of its history!

BIBLIOGRAPHY OF THE IMPORTANT BOOKS CONFIRMING THE ICELANDIC DISCOVERY OF AMERICA FROM THE YEARS 1076—1883.

1076. Adam von Bremen. "Historia Ecclesiastica Ecclesiarum Hamburgensis et Bremensis." Published in Copenhagen in 1579.
1570. Abraham Ortelius. "Theatrum Orbis Terrarum." English translation published in London in 1606.
1594. A Danish translation published of Snorre Sturleson's "Heimskringla." Copenhagen.
1611. Abraham Mylius. "Treatise de Antiquitate Linguæ Belgicæ." Leyden.
1642. Hugo Grotius. "Dissertatio de Origine Gentium Americanarum." Paris.
1705. Thormodus Torfæus. "Historia Vinlandiæ Antiquæ." Havniæ.
1755. Paul Henri Mallet. "Introduction à l'Histoire de Dannemarc." Copenhagen. Bishop Percy's English translation published in London in 1770. Title: "Northern Antiquities."
1767. David Cranz. "History of Greenland." London.
1773. Benjamin Franklin. Letter to Mr. Mather, in "Memoirs of the Life of, &c." London.
1777. Uno von Troil. "Letters on Iceland." Upsala.
1786. John Reinhold Forster. "History of the Voyages and Discoveries made in the North." London.
1808. John Pinkerton. "A general Collection of the best and most interesting Voyages and Travels in all parts of the World." London.
1810. "Annales des Voyages." Paris.
1811. Sir G. Steuart Mackenzie. "Travels in Iceland." Edinburgh.
1812. Hugh Williamson. "The History of North Carolina." Philadelphia.

1817. Conrad Malte-Brun. "Histoire de la Géographie." Paris.
1818. John Barrow. "A Chronological History of Voyages into the Arctic Regions." London.
1818. J. H. Shröeder. "Svea. Tidskrift för Vetenskap och Konst." Upsala.
1818. Eben. Henderson. "Iceland; or, the Journal of a Residence in that Island during the year 1814-15." Edinburgh.
1824. John V. N. Yates. "History of the State of New York." New York.
1825. Erik Gustaf Geijer. "Svea rikes häfder." Upsala.
1828. Washington Irving. "A History of the Life and Voyages of Christopher Columbus." London and New York.
1830. Henry Wheaton and Andrew Crichton. "Scandinavia, Ancient and Modern." Edinburgh.
1830. W. Cooley. "The History of Maritime and Inland Discovery." London.
1831. Henry Wheaton. "History of the Northmen, or Danes and Normans, from the earliest times to the Conquest of England by William of Normandy." London.
1831. W. Joseph Snelling. "The Polar Regions of the Western Continent Explored." Boston.
1833. Finn Magnusen. "Nordisk Tidsskrift for Oldkyndighet." Vol. II. Copenhagen.
1834. Josiah Priest. "American Antiquities and Discoveries in the West." Albany.
1834. T. Campanius. "Description of the Province of New Sweden." Philadelphia.
1836. Constantin Samuel Rafinesque. "The American Nations; or, Outlines of their General History, Ancient and Modern." Philadelphia.
1836. "Report addressed by the Royal Society of Northern Antiquaries to its British and American members." Copenhagen.
1837. Charles Christian Rafn. "Antiquitates Americanæ." Copenhagen.
1837. Wilhelm August Graah. "Narrative of an Expedition to the East Coast of Greenland . . . in search of the lost Colonies." London and Copenhagen.
1838. W. H. Prescott. "History of the reign of Ferdinand and Isabella." London and New York.
1838. *Foreign Quarterly Review.* London.
1838. Edward Everett. *North American Review.* Boston.
1838. *The Democratic Review.* Washington.
1838. *The New York Review.* New York.
1838. "The Royal Geographical Society." London.
1839. J. Toulmin Smith. "The Discovery of America by the Northmen." London.

1839. Grenville Pigott. "Scandinavian Mythology." London.
1841. N. L. Beamish. "The Discovery of America by the Northmen." London.
1842. K. Wilhelmi. "Island, Hvitramannaland, Grönland und Vinland, oder, der Normänner Leben auf Island und Grönland und deren Fahrten nach America schon über 500 Jahre vor Columbus."
1843. Th. H. Erslew. "Almindeligt Forfatter-Lexicon for Kongeriget Danmark." Vol. II., pp. 597—603.
1844. Samuel Laing. "Translation of the Heimskringla, with a preliminary Dissertation." London.
1844. Carl Heinrich Hermes. "Die Entdeckung von America durch die Isländer im zehnten und elften Jahrhunderte." Braunschweig.
1847. Alexander von Humboldt. "Cosmos." London.
1847. Gustaf Klemm. "Algemeine Cultur-Geschichte der Menschheit." Leipsig.
1850. "Ancient Scandinavia." In Chambers' Papers for the People. Vol. VI. Edinburgh.
1850. John T. Shillinglaw. "A Narrative of Arctic Discovery from the earliest period to the present time." London.
1852. Jens Jacob Asmussen Worsaae. "An account of the Danes and Norwegians in England, Scotland and Ireland." London.
1852. William and Mary Howitt. "The Literature and Romance of Northern Europe." London.
1852-54. A. E. Holmberg. "Nordbon under Hednatiden." Stockholm.
1854. Jacob Rudolph Keyser. "The Religion of the Northmen." London.
1854. Pliny Miles. "Nordurfari; or, Rambles in Iceland." New York.
1856. S. F. Haven. Smithsonian Institute. Washington.
1857. Charles Wyllys Elliott. "The New England History." New York.
1857. Oscar Ferdinand Peschel. "Geschichte des Zeitalters der Entdeckungen." Stuttgart.
1860. Georg Michael Asher. "Henry Hudson, the Navigator." London.
1860. Em. Domenech (L'abbé). "Seven Years' Residence in the Great Deserts of North America." London.
1860. Sir Charles Forbes. "Iceland; its Volcanoes, Geysers and Glaciers." London.
1862. Adamus Bremensis. "Menigheten i Norden, &c." Copenhagen.
1862. Andrew James Symington. "Pen and Pencil Sketches of Faröe and Iceland." London.
1863. Sabine Baring-Gould. "Iceland; its Scenes and Sagas." London.

1863. Désiré Charney and Viollet-Le-Duc. "Ruines Américaines." Paris.
1864. L. S. Borring. "Notices on the Life and Writings of Carl Christian Rafn." Copenhagen.
1865. Daniel Wilson. "Pre-Historic Man: Researches into the Origin of Civilization in the Old and the New World." London and Edinburgh.
1866. Paul C. Sinding. "History of Scandinavia, from the early times of the Northmen, the Sea-Kings and Vikings, to the present day." London.
1867. Hans Hildebrand. "Lifvet på Island i Sagotiden." Stockholm.
1868. Jacob Rudolph Keyser. "The Private Life of the Old Northmen." London.
1868. Carl Wilhelm von Paijkull. "A Summer in Iceland." London.
1868. B. F. De Costa. "The pre-Columbian Discovery of America by the Northmen." Albany.
1870. B. F. De Costa. "The Northmen in Maine." Albany.
1872. Cristoforo Colombo. "Select Letters." Translated and edited by R. H. Major. London.
1872. *Cornhill Magazine.* London.
1873. *National Quarterly Review.* New York.
1873. R. H. Major. "Voyages of the Zeni." London.
1874. Gabriel Gravier. "Découverte de l'Amerique par les Normands au Xe Siècle." Rouen and Paris.
1874. Aaron Goodrich. "A History of the Character and Achievements of the so-called Christopher Columbus." New York.
1874. Rasmus B. Anderson. "America not Discovered by Columbus." Chicago.
1875. Thomas Carlyle. "The Early Kings of Norway." London.
1875. Bayard Taylor. "Egypt and Iceland in the year 1874." London and New York.
1875. Hubert Howe Bancroft. "The Native Races of the Pacific States of North America." New York.
1875. Phineas Camp Headley. "The Island of Fire (Iceland); or, A Thousand Years of the Old Northmen's Home. 874-1874." Boston.
1875. J. T. Short. "The Galaxy." New York.
1875. Gilderoy Wells Griffen. "My Danish Days." Philadelphia.
1876. Marie A. Brown. "The Galaxy." New York.
1876-81. William Cullen Bryant and Sidney Howard Gay. "A Popular History of the United States, from the First Discovery of the Western Hemisphere." New York.
1876. Samuel Kneeland. "An American in Iceland." Boston.

1877. Alexander Farnum. "Visits of the Northmen to Rhode Island." Providence.
1877. Thomas Wentworth Higginson. "A Book of American Explorers." Boston.
1877. N. L. Beamish. "Voyages of the Northmen to America." Edited by E. F. Slafter. Boston.
1880. J. T. Short. "The North Americans of Antiquity." New York.
1880. Rev. F. Metcalfe. "The Englishman and the Scandinavian." London.
1880. G. H. Preble. "History of the Flag of the U.S.A., and the Flags of Ancient and Modern Nations." Boston.
1881. Frank Vincent, Jr. "Norsk, Lapp and Finns, &c." London and New York.
1881. P. B. Du Chaillu. "The Land of the Midnight Sun." London and New York.
1882. S. S. Cox. "Arctic Sunbeams." New York.
1883. Jules Leclercq. "La Terre de Glace." Paris.

www.ingramcontent.com/pod-product-compliance
Lightning Source LLC
Chambersburg PA
CBHW021820230426
43669CB00008B/816